The award-winning play

The Dead
Wait

By **Paul Herzberg**

This version of *The Dead Wait* was first performed
at Park Theatre on 6 November 2013

CAST

Lily Jozana	**Adelayo Adedayo**
George Jozana	**Maynard Eziashi**
Josh Gilmore	**Austin Hardiman**
Papa Louw	**Paul Herzberg**
Wambo Woman	**Adelayo Adedayo**

CREATIVE TEAM

Director	**Joe Harmston**
Producers	**Sarah Loader and Eleanor Rhode**
Designer	**Simon Scullion**
Lighting Designer	**Mike Robertson**
Original Composition and Sound Design	**Matthew Bugg**
Casting Director	**Kate Plantin CDG**
Costume Designer	**Holly Rose Henshaw**
Production Manager	**Will Mauchline**
Stage Manager	**Amy Slater**
Assistant Stage Manager	**Alice Barber**

Lighting Assistant	**Jack Weir**
Dresser	**Leah Curtis**
Assistant to the Producer	**Chris Snow**
Movement	**Simeon John Wake**
Set Construction	**Treend Construction Ltd**
Props Maker	**Anna Driftmier**
PR	**Kate Morley PR**
Online Promotions	**Chris McGill**
Production Artwork	**Keith Pattison / Rob Brown**
Pre-Production Artwork	**Steve Brannon**
Production Photographer	**Keith Pattison**

Special thanks to Diana Tyler, Hilary Best, Katie Harper and Stage One, Roger Carey, Anna Coombes, Sibu Mamba, Bronia Buchanan, Susan Smith, Nigel Godfrey, Amanda Evans, Alex Armitage, Charlie Ward and John Gilbert.

Paul Herzberg
Playwright
Playwright and actor Paul Herzberg served as a conscript during the time of the Angolan war. *The Dead Wait* is based, in part, on his experiences and the remarkable events connected to another soldier. It was shortlisted for the Verity Bargate Award; and on its UK premiere at The Royal Exchange received three *Manchester Evening News* Award nominations including Best New Play and Production, winning in the third category for Best Actor.

As a writer, Paul's theatre work includes *The Dead Wait*, *Where's The Bull?* (London Radio Writers Award), *Be Bop The Ruler* (*Time Out* Fringe First Nomination), *Sweet Like Suga* (Old Red Lion & Centaur Montreal), *Metropolis Kabarett* (National Theatre, co-writer), For BBC Radio *Dreaming Up Laura*, *The Song of My Father*, *The Crackwalker* and *The Wolf And Peter*; and for film, *Almost Heaven* (Nashville International Best Feature).

Joe Harmston
Director
Joe's theatre work has spanned a wide range of productions in London, across the UK, Europe and the USA, including Harold Pinter's *The Lover* and *The Collection* starring the writer (Donmar Warehouse) and Laurie Slade's *Joe & I* starring Peter Bowles (The King's Head). His most recent productions include the acclaimed reappraisal of Strindberg's *The Father* (The Belgrade, Coventry) and *The Prodigals* (UK Tour). Joe's focus on new writing has led him to work closely over long periods with playwrights including Harold Pinter, Sir Ronald Harwood, Sir Alan Ayckbourn, Sir David Hare, Sir Peter Ustinov as well as Laurie Slade, Paul Herzberg and Rod Dungate.

Simon Scullion
Set Designer
Simon trained at the Wimbledon School of Art, and was a Linbury Theatre Design finalist in 1993.

Simon's UK touring credits include *The Father*, *Murder on the Nile*, *The Haunting*, *Ben & Holly's Little Kingdom*, *Verdict*, *Witness for the Prosecution*, *If I Were You*, *Girl's Night Out*, *Lark Rise*, *Quartet*, *Spider's Web*, *Deceptions*, *Woman in Mind*, *Grass is Greener*, *Peppa Pig LIVE*, *Lazytown LIVE*, *I Do! I Do!*, *And Then There Were None*, *Quartermaine's Terms*, *Tons of Money*,

Sleuth, *Murder on Air Radio Plays*, *Elizabeth and Raleigh*, *The Unexpected Guest*, *Killer Joe* and *The Hollow*.

His West End and Off West End credits include *Eric and Little Ern* (Vaudeville), *Volcano* (Vaudeville Theatre), *The Leisure Society* (Trafalgar Studio), *Playing With Grown Ups* (Theatre 503), *Potted Potter* (Edinburgh, Vaudeville Theatre and Off Broadway), *What We Did To Weinstein* (Menier Chocolate Factory), *Joe and I* (The King's Head), *How to Lose Friends and Alienate People* (The Arts Theatre), *Murderer* (Menier Chocolate Factory), *Fair Maid of the West* (Pleasance Theatre), *Zipp!* (Duchess Theatre), *My Sainted Aunt* (New End Theatre), *The Proceedings of that Night* (Director, Pleasance).
His collaboration with Joe Harmston began in 2001 at the Palace Theatre, Westcliffe, where Simon created the design for the inaugural Agatha Christie Festival. This later became the Agatha Christie Theatre Company, who present an annual touring production, which Simon and Joe continue to collaborate on.

Mike Robertson
Lighting Designer
In 2007 Mike was the winner of the Olivier Award for Best Lighting Design for his work on *Sunday in the Park with George* (Menier Chocolate Factory and Wyndhams Theatre). In 2010 he was nominated for a WhatsOnStage Award for his design for *On The Waterfront* (Theatre Royal Haymarket).
Mike's collaborations with Joe Harmston, Simon Scullion and Matthew Bugg include *The Father* (Belgrade Theatre, Coventry), *Murder on the Nile* (UK Tour), *Verdict* (UK Tour) and *Larkrise to Candleford* (UK Tour).
Recent credits include *Volcano* (Vaudeville Theatre and UK Tour), *Funny Peculiar* (UK Tour), *Dry Rot* (UK Tour), *The Billie Holiday Story* (Charing Cross Theatre), *Parade* (Old Vic Tunnels), *Gibraltar* (Arcola Theatre), *Fragile* (Belgrade Theatre, Coventry), *Dear World* (Charing Cross Theatre), *Riccardo Primo* (Royal College of Music), *The Producers* (Arts Ed), *Six Actors in Search of a Director* (Charing Cross Theatre, Directed by Steven Berkoff), *Death & Gardening* (UK Tour, Edinburgh Festival), *Oedipus* (Nottingham Playhouse and Edinburgh Festival), *Third Floor* (Trafalgar Studios), *Company* (Southwark Playhouse), *Billy Liar* (West Yorkshire Playhouse), *Cabaret* (Wilton's Music Hall), *Guys & Dolls* (Cambridge Arts Theatre), *Educating Rita* (Watermill Theatre, Newbury), *Wolfboy* (George Square

Theatre, Edinburgh), *New Boy* (Trafalgar Studios), *Hair* (English Theatre, Frankfurt), *Too Close to the Sun* (Comedy Theatre), *My Fair Lady* (Cambridge Arts Theatre), *Anything Goes* (Cambridge Arts Theatre), *Five Guys Named Moe* (English Theatre, Frankfurt), *Sunday in the Park With George* (Menier Chocolate Factory and Wyndhams Theatre), *Othello* (Birmingham Stage Company), *Sit and Shiver* directed by Steven Berkoff (Hackney Empire), *Deathtrap* (English Theatre, Frankfurt), *Seesaw* (Arts Ed), *The Spring Proms* (Royal Albert Hall), *Fascinating Aida* (UK Tour), *The Glee Club* (Bolton Octagon and Cochrane Theatre) and *The Wood Demon* (Playhouse Theatre).

Matthew Bugg
Sound Design and Original Composition
Matthew has written and produced *Miss Nightingale*, a new musical set in London 1942. The critically acclaimed piece has now toured the UK twice, and has also played in the West End. His collaborations with Joe Harmston, Simon Scullion and Mike Robertson include *The Father* (The Belgrade, Coventry), *Murder on the Nile*, *Verdict* and *Lark Rise to Candleford*.
His other work includes: *Volcano*, *Three Men In a Boat*, *Go Back for Murder, The Secret of Sherlock Holmes* (West End), *The Handyman*, *Barefoot in the Park*, *Alarms and Excursions*, *Star Quality*, *Quartet*, *The Hound of the Baskervilles*, *My Brilliant Divorce*, *Northanger Abbey*, *Jamaica Inn*, *Angelina Ballerina* (UK Tours), *The League of Youth*, *All Quiet on the Western Front*, *To Reach the Clouds*, *Because It's There*, *The Mill on the Floss*, *Wonderful Tennessee*, *Polygraph* (Nottingham Playhouse), *The Invention of Love*, *Barbarians*, *Secret Rapture* (Salisbury Playhouse), *Vanity Fair* (Northcott, Exeter), *Northanger Abbey*, *Amadeus* (Theatre Royal York), *A Family Affair*, *Double Indemnity*, *The Glass Menagerie* (New Wolsey, Ipswich), *Rumpelstiltskin*, *Great Expectations*, *Duck!* (Unicorn Theatre), *A Perfect Ganesh*, *The True Life Fiction of Mata Hari* (Palace, Watford), *Richard III*, *Don Juan on Trial*, *The Provok'd Wife*, *Uncle Vanya* (Mercury theatre, Colchester), *The Canterbury Tales* (Northern Broadsides UK Tour), *The Firebird* (Bolton, Octagon), *Little Wolf's Book of Badness* (Hampstead), *The Impostor* (Plymouth Theatre Royal). Matthew also performed the role of Ariel in *The Tempest* for Nottingham Playhouse.

Kate Plantin CDG
Casting Director
Kate's theatre credits include *Kindertransport* (UK Tour), *Storm in a Flower Vase* (Arts Theatre), *The Handyman* (UK Tour), *The Father* (Belgrade, Coventry), *Of Mice and Men* (UK Tour), *Touching the Blue* (Edinburgh), *Lone Star and Private Wars* (Kings Head), *Marilyn and Ella* (Edinburgh and London), *On the Island of* Aars (Edinburgh), *Joan Rivers – A Work in Progress* (Edinburgh and London), *Telstar* which Kate also co-produced in the West End and for which Con O'Neill was nominated for an Olivier Award for his portrayal of Joe Meek, *Road to Nirvana* (King's Head), *The Trestle at Pope Lick Creek* (Southwark and Manchester Royal Exchange), *On Your Toes* (Royal Festival Hall) and *Follies* (Royal Festival Hall). Kate's film credits include *Squat* (Scanner-Rhodes), *Index Zero* (Margherita Films), *Gone Too Far* (Poisson Rouge), *Outpost: Rise of the Spetsnaz* (Black Camel), *The Timber* (ANA Media), *Le Weekend* (Poisson Rouge), *Outpost: Black Sun* (Black Camel), *The Wicker Tree* (British Lion), *Siren* (Poisson Rouge), *The Hide* (Poisson Rouge), *Walled In* (Leomax), *Book of Blood* (Matador), *Princess Ka'iulani* (Matador), *Telstar: The Joe Meek Story* (Aspiration Films), *City Rats* (Face Films), *Outpost* (Black Camel), *Senseless* (Matador), *Turistas* (Eagle Pictures), *Seed of Chucky* (Rogue Pictures), *Chaos and Cadavers* (Matador) and *Another Life* (Alibi).

Holly Rose Henshaw
Costume Designer
Holly trained at the Central School of Speech and Drama. Her work varies from set and costume design, to fashion design, illustration and installations.
For Snapdragon Productions, Holly was Costume Designer for *Thark* (Park Theatre) and *A Life* (Finborough Theatre). Previous work includes *Untitled 13* (in production with Thin Man Films), *Spring Awakening* (Central School of Speech and Drama), the Olympic and Paralympic Opening and Closing Ceremonies, *Landance South West Olympic Festival 2012, Accidental Festival 2012* (Roundhouse), *True Stories* (BBC2), *The Kitchen* (National Theatre), *Transformation and Revelation* (Prague Design Quadrennial 2011), *Beanfield* (Bike Shed Theatre, Exeter) and *Rhinoceros* (Northcott Theatre, Exeter).

Sarah Loader
Producer

In addition to working as the lead Producer on all of Snapdragon's productions, Sarah has recently worked alongside Simon McBurney on the development of two new opera productions in association with the Netherlands State Opera and English National Opera: Mozart's *The Magic Flute* (2012/2013) and *A Dog's Heart* (2011/2012) which was presented in February 2013 at Theatro Alla Scala, Milan.

Sarah is a former Production Executive for Bill Kenwright, where she looked after the West End productions of *Blood Brothers* and *The Pitmen Painters* (co-production with the National Theatre and Live Theatre Newcastle) and amongst others, the touring productions of Andrew Lloyd Webber's *Joseph and the Amazing Technicolor Dreamcoat* and *Starlight Express*, as well as the annual collaboration between Bill Kenwright and the Agatha Christie Theatre Company, led by Joe Harmston.

Sarah was the fundraising officer for the Finborough Theatre and founded the venue's annual new writing festival, 'Vibrant!', now in its fourth year.

Sarah originally trained as a musician at Durham University before completing an MA in Advanced Theatre Practice (Producing) at Central School of Speech and Drama.

Eleanor Rhode
Artistic Director for Snapdragon Productions

Eleanor Rhode trained at Mountview and the National Theatre Studio as a Director before forming Snapdragon Productions in 2009.

In 2013, Eleanor was nominated for an Off West End Award (Best Direction) for *Thark* at Park Theatre.

Her directing work for Snapdragon includes: *Thark* (Park Theatre), *A Life* and the London premieres of *Time Out* Critics' Choice productions of *The Drawer Boy* and *Generous* (Finborough Theatre). Other directing includes *The Gypsy Thread* (National Theatre Studio),
The Error of Their Ways (Cockpit Theatre), *A Number* (Camden People's Theatre), *This Lime Tree Bower* (Edinburgh Festival) and staged readings of *The Promised Land* (Tristan Bates), *The Geese of Beverly Road* (Theatre503), *Photos of You Sleeping* (Hampstead Theatre) and *100 Men*, The *December Man* (*L'homme de décembre*), *Sihanoukville* and *Barrow Hill* (Finborough Theatre).

 As Associate Director, she has worked on the London transfer of *Lie of The Land* (Arcola Theatre).

Eleanor is a former Staff Director at the National Theatre.

Adelayo Adedayo
Lily Jozana / Wambo Woman
Adelayo trained at the Identity School of Acting and *The Dead Wait* marks her stage debut.
For television, her work includes the leading role of Viva in *Some Girls* (BBC), *M.I. High*, *Skins* and *Meet The Bandais*. For film, her work includes *Gone Too Far* (which premieres at this year's London Film Festival), *Sket* and *Family Legacy*.

Maynard Eziashi
George Jozana
Maynard's stage credits include *Wedlock of the Gods* (Cochrane Theatre), *Quay West* (Burghtheatre, Vienna), *One Mile Away, The Winter's Tale, Pericles* (RSC), *Guess Who's Coming For Dinner* (St Andrew's Lane Theatre, Dublin), *A Jamaican Airman Forsees His Death* (Royal Court), *The Island* (Citizens Band) and *A Respectable Wedding* (Almeida).
For television, his work includes *Hotel Babylon, The Captain, Bad Boys, The Changeling, Downtown Lagos* and *Hallelujah Anyhow*.
For film, his work includes *Paradise or Something, Saidi's Song, The Contract, Colour Me Kubrick, Anansi, Kiss Kiss Bang Bang, Ace Ventura Pet Detective II, A Good Man in Africa, Bopha* and *Mr Johnson* (for which he won the Silver Bear award for Best Actor at the Berlin Film Festival).

Austin Hardiman
Josh Gilmore
Austin was born in South Africa, trained at The Waterfront Theatre School, Cape Town and Drama Studio, London, and has been based in London since 2001.
His stage credits include *Twelfth Night, A Midsummer Night's Dream* (Antic Disposition), *The Window Cleaner, Macbeth* (Faction Theatre) and *True West* (Jermyn Street Theatre).
For television, his work includes *Dancing On the Edge*; and for film, his work includes *False Murder, Somnambulant, Phyllis, Sorrows* (which won the Special Jury Award at The 2013 Worldfest Houston International Film Festival), *Forget Me Not* and *The Dark Room*.

Paul Herzberg
Papa Louw

Paul's stage credits include *The Doctor's Dilemma* (National Theatre), *The Taming Of The Shrew* (RSC), *A Streetcar Named Desire* (Mermaid), *Dancing At Lughnasa* (Abbey Dublin), *The Merchant Of Venice* (Arcola), *ID* (Almeida), *While The Sun Shines, People Are Living There, Romeo And Juliet, Arms And The Man, The Dead Wait* (Royal Exchange), *The Merchant Of Venice, Carrington* (Chichester), *Oleanna* (Scarborough), *The Grapes Of Wrath* (Birmingham Rep), *Sweet Like Suga* (Centaur Montreal).

For television, his work includes *The Honourable Woman, Spooks, The Life And Loves Of A She Devil, Murder City, Inspector Lynley, Band Of Brothers, Heartbeat* and *Lovejoy*.

For film, his work includes *My Week With Marilyn, Papadopolous & Sons, The Book Of Eve, Blood, Cry Freedom* and *Almost Heaven*.

About Park Theatre

With two theatres, a learning suite, a café bar and a gallery, London's newest venue is fully accessible and pleasantly air-conditioned! So, please make Park Theatre your regular home from home – and visit us again... and again!

We are very grateful to all the individuals and corporations who have made generous donations to help us meet the costs of building the state-of-the-art theatre complex that you are in today. However, the finances of running a theatre of this scale are such that ticket sales alone cannot cover our costs. With no money from the Arts Council we need support to fund ongoing expenditure and enable us to stage high-quality productions.

We have launched a number of schemes including: becoming a Friend, naming a seat, sponsoring a production and legacy giving. The benefits for donors range from priority booking to corporate entertainment. So, whether you would like to donate as little as ten pounds, fund a complete production or something in between, we would be delighted to hear from you! Thank you.

Jez Bond, Artistic Director
info@parktheatre.co.uk

For Park Theatre

Staff

SNAPDRAGON PRODUCTIONS

Executive Producer | **Sarah Loader**
Artistic Director | **Eleanor Rhode**
Business Director | **Pelham Olive**

Snapdragon Productions was formed by Producer Sarah Loader and Artistic Director Eleanor Rhode in 2009 to bring neglected and unknown works to new audiences. In 2012, Snapdragon became a limited company under the direction of Pelham Olive, and won the Stage One Bursary for New Producers.

The Dead Wait marks Snapdragon's return to the Park Theatre following their multi-award nominated production of *Thark* by Ben Travers. The revival was the first London production in nearly 30 years, and the world premiere of its new adaptation by Clive Francis.

Productions development include *A Bill of Divorcement* by Clemence Dane, *Four Places* by Joel Drake Johnson, a trilogy of plays by Lanford Wilson and a new commission with the playwright and screenwriter Al Smith.

Other previous productions include the revival of *A Life* by Hugh Leonard, the London premiere of Michael Healey's *The Drawer Boy* which was named *Time Out* Critics' Choice, the world premiere of *Barrow Hill* by Jane Wainwright, the European premiere of Michael Healey's *Generous* which enjoyed two sell-out runs and was also named *Time Out* Critics' Choice, the award-winning European premiere of Rodgers and Hammerstein's musical *Me and Juliet* (all Finborough Theatre) and *Anna Karenina* (Arcola Theatre). Snapdragon co-produced the world premiere of Anders Lustgarten's *A Day at the Racists* (Finborough Theatre and the Broadway Theatre, Barking) which was nominated for the 2010 TMA Award for Outstanding Achievement in Regional Theatre and won the playwright the Inaugural Harold Pinter Award for Playwriting.

www.snapdragonproductions.com

If you would like to join our Friends mailing list please email Sarah on info@snapdragonproductions.com

 Snapdragon Productions is grateful for the support and mentoring received through Stage One

Snapdragon Productions Ltd. is a registered limited company. Registered company number: 7923298. Registered office: Brook Henderson House, 37-43 Blagrave Street, Reading, RG1 1PZ

Paul Herzberg

THE DEAD WAIT

OBERON BOOKS
LONDON

WWW.OBERONBOOKS.COM

First published in 2002 by Oberon Books Ltd
521 Caledonian Road, London N7 9RH
Tel: +44 (0) 20 7607 3637 / Fax: +44 (0) 20 7607 3629
e-mail: info@oberonbooks.com
www.oberonbooks.com

A catalogue record for this book is available from the British
Library.

PB ISBN: 978-1-84002-342-8
E ISBN: 978-1-78319-459-9

Cover design by Keith Pattison and Rob Brown

Printed and bound by Marston Book Services Limited., Didcot..

Visit www.oberonbooks.com to read more about all our books
and to buy them. You will also find features, author interviews and
news of any author events, and you can sign up for e-newsletters
so that you're always first to hear about our new releases.

Contents

For my parents, Lily and Bernhard
in whom the passion for a better world
stayed undiminished till the end.

With special thanks to:

Diana Tyler (for her unwavering belief in the play); my constant family: Oona, Jenni and Tom; Vincent Ebrahim; Clare Stopford (for her dedication when it was produced at The Market); David Clough; The RNT Studio; Marius Van Niekerk; Andy Jordan (for a splendid production on BBC Radio 4); Paul Sirett and the Soho Theatre; James Hogan at Oberon; Jacob Murray (for his tenacity when it was staged at The Royal Exchange); Bernhard Herzberg and Lily Herzberg – my late parents; Joe Harmston for his integrity and determination to see a London production of the play; Pelham Olive and the two whirlwinds: Sarah Loader and Eleanor Rhode of Snapdragon Productions.

The Dead Wait

The Dead Wait was shortlisted for the 1996 Verity Bargate Award and produced at the Market Theatre Johannesburg, the same year. The play had its British premiere at the Royal Exchange in 2002, nominated for three *Manchester Evening News* Awards: Best Play, Production and Actor – winning in the last category.

Please note:
The original published version of the play (2002)
has now undergone a further draft (2013).

feel it rip through the guts and snatch a ball en route. The effect is telling. Our men scream out as one. My skin opens up like a flower and offers us a view of my bones. Then, transfixed by the hole, we are silent.

(Beat.)

The shell has pierced a Coca-Cola sign emblazoned on the wall of our shack. Through the gap I see children skidding in the dust as my saviours enter the clearing: a battalion of white soldiers with a madman in command. No one reaches the bush alive. *(Imitating Papa.) 'Shoot the runners, torture the stayers!'* That is his rule. Five men, three women and a goat. But for him, it's a lucky day. Inside that shack is the catch of a lifetime: ANC operative on recce from London: *(Smiles.)* Me.

(Beat.)

I wake up on the back of the runner, moving by night through the bush…to find that pain has new meaning. But through it all I feel his power. A boy in the body of a Samson. And somewhere, within him, a strange nobility.

We talk. And talk. And talk… And in that madness, somehow, between me and him, a link, thin as spit has been made. – I pray for sleep. None comes. There is a blessing. My wound is clean. Though so much blood. And a rich indigo that intrigues me… Let's face it, comrades… I'm dead!

MARIMBA start and build.

Yet…suspended in this place. A place of neglect, of oblivion, of…limbo. And here I am, shackled in time. And I wait. And wait… Queuing for a bus is bad enough, but this is something else, I can tell you. To flit about as a tormented spirit for twenty years without a change of clothes. And I wait, in hope…

The MARIMBA peak and fade quickly.

I wait…for the return of the runner.

BLACKOUT.

SCENE TWO

A graveside. Cape Town. The present. Dim light. WIND. Then a snappy INTRO JINGLE:

PRESENTER 2: *(African)* Metro Radio FM 96.7! For those of you with long memories, a former sporting icon has returned at last to the troubled shores of our rainbow nation. *Who the hell is Josh Gilmore I hear you say?* Well now…this is the man they called *'The Blur'*.

> *JOSH, now in his late 30s, dressed in a suit, strobed by FLASHBULBS, approaches, a spade in his hand.*

His exit from Green Point stadium straight into exile more than twenty years ago marked one of the strangest sporting events of all time. But today he's back. Here, to bury the man who trained him. *His father.*

> *JOSH heaps soil into a grave. He seems detached.*

Who knows what might have been with this once great athlete and what drove him to destroy a life of privilege, his god-given talent and the hopes and dreams of the white society that spawned him.

> *JOSH removes an army kit bag from the grave. A last FLASHBULB POPS plunging everything but JOSH into darkness. JOSH unzips the bag. MARIMBA… He gingerly reaches inside and remove his kit: uniform, boots, webbing, metal plates, steel helmet, survival knife…until he finds the final item: a folded, bloodied cloth. The MARIMBA intensify.*

> *JOSH unwraps the cloth to reveal a crudely carved figurine: a WOODEN SOLDIER with rifle, saluting. He holds the figurine up to the light. The MARIMBA hit crescendo then cut dead.*

> *There is the sound of an AMPLIFIED STOPWATCH as PAPA LOUW emerges from the darkness, the phantom of Josh's nightmares – JOSH is frozen at the sight of him. PAPA is in mid 40s, a still, brooding, presence, dressed in the 'nutria browns' of the South African Defence Force, the three pips of a Captain on his epaulettes. After ten seconds he clicks*

his fingers cutting the STOPWATCH DEAD. PAPA does not take his eyes off JOSH. Finally, PAPA turns to the audience.

PAPA: *Time* – is not an issue with everyone, I admit. But to me it's the essence of it all. How long does it take a sperm to pierce an egg? – Two seconds. *Bang!* There's a life. Last century, hey? – Stalin, Hitler, Saddam – Six seconds. And those men, what did they do? They stole it. They stole time. Millions of people were fucked by those random seconds. – *Chance* – 'A force to cause events that cannot be foreseen.'

> *(Beat.)*

Twenty years ago. Me and him. We were in the army, together. We went on a holiday. An Angolan holiday. It was something. How much life is in twenty years *when two seconds creates one.*

> *(Beat.)*

You know, one of the things I pride myself in is my power of recollection. Things that happened when I was two years old are crystal clear to me. It's a bit of an affliction. Because memory is fixed to emotion. And I am an emotional man. *'I saw under the sun, that the race is not to the swift, nor the battle to the strong, but time and chance happeneth to them all.'* – Ecclesiastes. – We *all* have secrets. Some people find them hard to live with. To confess. I don't.

> *(Beat.)*

I can adapt. That's my talent. Ma used to say you could put me in Paraguay with sixpence and I'd be the local sheriff in a month. I seldom think about the past. Once upon a time I was in the army. It's a long time ago. Last century is over and when Christ turned two thousand I was fifty-six. Things have happened to me. That's good. You can't be a man with no pain in your heart. When I do look back… which is rare these days. I see young men in an adventure. I see history.

He turns to JOSH.

29

Because that's what it is.

He turns back to the audience.

And that's where it should stay.

> *PAPA disappears into darkness as LILY JOZANA steps from it.*
> *JOSH remains still, staring at her intently. LILY is impassive*
> *– she stands, arms folded, observing him. JOSH turns away*
> *from LILY and faces the audience.*

JOSH: It's all gone now and hallelujah to that: commissions of
truth, the crocodile tears of killers spouting the new-speak
of our so-called rainbow nation, hand-wringing liberals
bleating behind their ramparts.

(Pause.)

Twenty years ago, I met a man. In the few days I knew
him, I learned about living. Around me was death. His
name was George Jozana.

He turns back to LILY.

Your father.

> *MARIMBA TINKLE. The spot fades on JOSH. Somewhere in*
> *the darkness, GEORGE watches LILY.*

LILY: By the time I was ten I spoke four languages. Russian,
German, English and Czech. The one that defied me,
mother tongue of my ancestors, was Zulu. To be foreign,
to be the child of an exile in Moscow and Prague in the
eighties was something of a challenge to a little black girl.
But they say kids can function in any setting. And I did. I
functioned.

(Beat.)

Not so my mother. Shunted to places she loathed into
cultures she failed to grasp, peeping into dark corners for
fear of execution and married to a man whose every word
the exile collective took as holy scripture. After she leapt
off a high-rise when I was five there was just us. The sage
and his kid. He was beautiful. He was the most loving
father a child ever had. But he was fleeting as twilight. A

fact often omitted from the tales of our deliverance is that most of its heroes were married to the struggle.

>*(Beat.)*

There was one place us children of exile feared most – because we knew the rate of return. And on my tenth birthday, the only time I ever saw him cry, he said it:

GEORGE: *Lily sithandwa sami, ngiya e-Angola.*

LILY: *(Translating.)* Lily, my love, I am going to Angola.

>*BLACKOUT.*

>*The SOUNDS of a NAMIBIAN BORDER MILITARY CAMP begin to envelop us.*

ACT TWO

SCENE ONE

<u>Ondangwa military camp, Northern Namibia</u>. The past. Three months before Josh's shock exit from the stadium. CICADAS. Blazing sun. Ochre earth. JOSH, in SADF uniform, is pacing with his R4 rifle on guard duty. He is fresh-faced, luminous with life. A shock of golden fringe peeps from beneath his bush hat. There is the SOUND OF A HELICOPTER GUNSHIP bursting into the airspace above. JOSH watches its flight path – then to Billy Joel's 'We Didn't Start The Fire' using his rifle as a guitar – he starts to sing:

JOSH: Harry Truman, Doris Day, Red China, Johnnie Ray…

> *He completes the first verse and chorus. PAPA enters unseen – and watches as JOSH Chuck Berry's his way across the stage, reworking the lyrics for the second verse:*

Johnny Vorster, Malenkov, Botha and Prokofiev
Rockefeller, Old Mandela, Communist Bloc,
Boycott, smack my bot, Cindy Crawford, shit she's hot
Dien Bien, fuck falls, 'Rock Around the Clock'
Einstein, James Dean, Cape Town's got a winning team
Davy Crockett, Dollar Brand, Zulu impi, Disneyland,
Botha, Old Nick, Dolly Parton, suck my dick,
Princess Grace, white race, trouble in the townships
> *(He sings the second chorus ending in:)*
But we tried to fight it… –

> *JOSH sees PAPA, freezes, stands to attention and salutes.*

JOSH: Sir!

PAPA: Singing on guard duty. Good sign. I like to see a soldier who's relaxed in the action area.

> *PAPA is motionless. JOSH is bemused. He drops his salute and stands at ease, rifle by his side.*

Lucky?

PAPA offers JOSH a cigarette from a pack of Lucky Strike. JOSH hesitates.

Go on. Take.

JOSH does. PAPA lights it for him. JOSH inhales.

I can't help feeling we've met. You get that with some people.

PAPA studies JOSH.

I know what it is. You remind me of this posh boy who pitched up in my squad. Once fucked five girls between Friday night and Sunday lunch. Could march a whole day without breaking sweat. Crack shot with a rifle. Clever as fuck. You know the type. Even his shit smelt good.

JOSH laughs.

What a poes.

JOSH: My shits are *lethal*, sir.

PAPA: Thing was. The moment he got into battle? Cried for his mommy.

JOSH: Then you're dead right, sir. Sounds a prize poes.

PAPA: Tell me something I don't know.

JOSH: Hey? – *Sorry…*'sir.'

PAPA: Tell me something I don't know.

JOSH is perplexed, but being JOSH, he chances it:

JOSH: What's the height of conceit?

(Beat.)

Calling out your own name when you cum.

PAPA does not react.

Okay. What do you call a bunny with a bent cock?

(Beat.)

'Fucks funny.'

PAPA: I'm waiting.

JOSH: I don't know what you want, sir.

PAPA: Tell me something I don't know.

JOSH: Is that because you're bored, sir?

PAPA: Tell me something I don't know you smug fuck or I'll shove your pretty blonde head up your arse.

JOSH: The guys in the unit are scared of you.

>*PAPA grips JOSH in a chokehold.*

PAPA: *Tell me something I don't know!*

JOSH: *(Finally blurting it out through blocked breath.)* I'm not.

PAPA: *(Releasing him.)* Good. That's a *start.*

>*JOSH massages his throat and catches his breath, trying to regain composure, now more wary. PAPA clicks his fingers: there is the magnified SOUND OF A STOPWATCH. PAPA counts silently. He clicks his fingers again: The sound cuts dead.*

That's how long it took to run the hundred in eighteen ninety-eight. If you study the records it's dropped two seconds in ninety years. Two seconds over that distance is twenty meters. Put that Greek against Paul Nash now it's how far behind he'd be at the tape. Blows my mind. No white sprinter has held the world record since the war. But two decades back Nash equalled it. A South African. Ten seconds. Man against the clock. Forget the four-minute mile. *(Imitates a sprinter in full flight, in slow-motion.)*

PAPA: This is flying. The human body at thirty miles an hour. Man, sort of…touching god.

>*PAPA waits for some sort of reaction – but JOSH appears, quite simply, to be perplexed. PAPA sighs.*

Way back when I read the officers' 'Training Manual' it said: 'Talk *to* the men not *with* them.' I thought about that. Not a good thing to do in the army, is it? *Think.* But I did. And I reckoned if I was in the bush with a bloke who could save my life and he was someone I'd never *looked in the eye* – he might think twice.

>*Again PAPA seems to be demanding a response; again, there is nothing. PAPA does an imaginary gun draw.*

JOSH smiles at *GEORGE* in relief, turns – and throws up on *PAPA's* boots. *GEORGE* laughs. – <u>*For a second*</u> <u>*GEORGE's eyes meet JOSH's and something passes between*</u> <u>*them*</u> *– a joint awareness of the absurdity of the moment. PAPA takes this in, silent…still.*

PAPA: Carry him.

JOSH: Hey?

PAPA: Carry. Him.

JOSH: Where to, sir?

PAPA: Back.

JOSH: Back?

PAPA: To the border.

JOSH: Why?

PAPA: Interrogation.

JOSH emits a short, shrill laugh.

JOSH: Holy cock.

JOSH: And you?

PAPA: Guard. Watchdog.

(Beat.)

Wet nurse. – You'll need me. But I need to move. I'll find you.

JOSH: Perfect. Snazzy. And at night?

PAPA: Southern Cross, city boy, to guide you back.

JOSH: The border!

(Beat.)

How far's that…sir…?

PAPA: Fifty K. Or we can leave him here to die. Your choice.

(Beat.)

'Champ.'

BLACKOUT.

MARIMBA – TRAVELLING THEME.

SCENE FOUR

The bush, southern Angola. Predawn. CICADAS. In the dim light a giant is moving. The giant is singing 'Knockin' on Heaven's Door' between deep breaths. There is the distant sound of AK-47 MACHINE-GUN FIRE. A spot picks up GEORGE on JOSH's back. They seem to be moving towards us.

JOSH: *Ma takes this badge off'a me*

> *JOSH completes the first verse of 'Knockin' on Heaven's Door'.*

GEORGE: *(In pain, right into JOSH's ear.) Badimo…!*

JOSH: Now what?

GEORGE: Amadlozi Badimo…

JOSH: Christ.

GEORGE: Every step you take…*it rips me open.*

JOSH: So…you speak English.

GEORGE: Yes.

> *JOSH stops moving.*

JOSH: Then listen to me.

GEORGE: Yes?

JOSH: *Shut up!*

> *JOSH moves off quickly. GEORGE looks around.*

GEORGE: Where is he?

JOSH: No, man.

GEORGE: Where! Your commander!

JOSH: What'd I just say?

GEORGE: The place…

JOSH: Hey?!

GEORGE: The place of battle!

JOSH: All right, man! The place what?

GEORGE: Just me? Who was left? Just me?

JOSH: Look, buddy. I don't know you. I don't owe you anything, right?

GEORGE: I'm a man, much older than you. Just a captive, boy, in your covert war.

Sound of DISTANT GUNFIRE. JOSH stops, dead still.

JOSH: Want to fucking know do you? It was like a run through hell! And Papa? – Haven't got a bloody clue.

GEORGE: Papa?

JOSH: Our boys, they…fucked off. Vanished. Into nowhere. After we'd burned the place. All that's fucking left of us is me and him. Till we found you.

JOSH starts to move again.

Just you alive in that place – what's left of it.

GEORGE: 'Shut up.'

JOSH: What!?

GEORGE: 'Shut up.' That's what you said.

JOSH: What I said *then*!

GEORGE: 'A run through hell'?

JOSH: So zip it.

They move on in silence. GEORGE grimaces.

GEORGE: I need to…to piss. I need…

JOSH: Then piss. Can't stop. Each time I do it's hell to start up again.

GEORGE: *Did your parents ever talk to you of manners, boy?*

JOSH: Go on then. Piss, man. *SO PISS!*

GEORGE: *Aaaargghhh…*nothing…comes, nothing…why?

JOSH: Please, man.

GEORGE: *Tell me!*

JOSH: Please…

GEORGE: I need to know.

JOSH: What?

GEORGE: The harm.

JOSH: To what?

GEORGE: *My body.* You saw…

JOSH: Saw what, man?

GEORGE: The wounds.

JOSH: Not your mouth. That still works.

GEORGE: Tell me.

JOSH: I can't fucking talk and carry you, man!

> *JOSH loses his footing and stumbles.*

GEORGE: *AAAARRGGHHH!*

JOSH: Jesus! You lost some of your…equipment man, your ball and… I'm not a medic…

GEORGE: I lost *what?…*

JOSH: Sorry, man.

GEORGE: *Amadlozi badimo!*

> *JOSH tries to focus, controlling his breath like an athlete.*

JOSH: *Ma, take this badge off'a me…*

> *JOSH completes the first verse of 'Knockin' on Heaven's Door'.*

GEORGE: Teach me.

JOSH: Now what?

GEORGE: This song…this tune.

JOSH: Hey?

GEORGE: This thing you hum.

JOSH: Heaven's Door. Knockin' On… Heaven's Door?

GEORGE: Teach me…

PAPA: *(Offstage.)* Drop him.

SCENE FIVE

A bush clearing. A stifling, late Angolan afternoon. PAPA enters and watches as JOSH staggers in. GEORGE is unconscious on his back.

JOSH: Can't move...another inch, sir, not another inch.

> *GEORGE moans.*

Christ...we're stuck together. Hang on man.

> *JOSH shakes GEORGE free laying him down gently.*
>
> *PAPA is fascinated by the care JOSH is taking.*

There...got to sit.

> *JOSH rubs the small of his back. His shirt is bloodied.*

Where were you, sir!

> *PAPA takes a banana from his pocket and throws it to JOSH. JOSH eyes it hungrily.*

How the hell did you get that?

> *JOSH rips into the banana. PAPA faces GEORGE.*

PAPA: So...what's a nice girl like you doing in a place like this?

> *GEORGE refuses eye contact.*

Why were you in that village?

> *Still, GEORGE doesn't look up. PAPA whistles at him. GEORGE turns away.*

The Fifth Amendment doesn't work in the bush.

> *PAPA strikes GEORGE in the face – GEORGE's spectacles fly off. – PAPA picks the glasses up. He examines the stems.*

'Dolland And... Atchison, Ox...ford Street.' Private... You think the Wambo people shop in London?

JOSH: *(Mouth filled with banana.)* Sir...we're on foreign soil, sir. Shouldn't we first...get him back?

PAPA: I've been around local tribes for twenty years. And I don't agree with my colleagues. There *is* a difference between some of you. I'd say...you were not from this region. I'd guess...you are not from this country. In fact,

I'd stake my life that you are one of my…fellow citizens.
One of Mandela's mob. So *what* are you doing *here?*
There's no negotiation.

PAPA walks to the spectacles.

Answer the question. Or face the music.

PAPA crushes the spectacles with his boot.

Private Gilmore can tell you the tune I play.

PAPA walks towards the bush –

Stay with him, private. I need some air. That wound's
starting to stink.

JOSH: *Don't go…* Sir.

PAPA stops – JOSH's plaintive tone seems to have got to him.

PAPA: You a lucky man, Private. You serving your country.
Makes you a hero. What you are back home, isn't it? A
hero?

PAPA moves off again.

JOSH: Please!

PAPA stops then walks up to JOSH.

PAPA: Head south. *This is what you trained for.* The enemy left
us a plum. Our friend's no Wambo. Forget all that crap
about winning 'hearts.' We just get back to base and on
route find out what's in that foul black 'mind.'

JOSH stares back at him, blankly.

This country's my back yard. I'll be circling like the sun.
(With sudden inexplicable tenderness.) You won't lose me
troopie.

PAPA reaches out and touches JOSH's cheek.

PAPA: Ever.

PAPA exits. JOSH stares at the ground.

GEORGE: He… *(A spasm of pain grips him.)* he…

JOSH kneels and looks at the wound.

JOSH: I can't do anything more for you, man. Here.

He unstraps his water bottle, checks the coast is clear.

Quickly!

GEORGE takes a few sips, stares at JOSH.

GEORGE: He needs your approval.

JOSH: Needs what?

GEORGE: Needs you to need him.

JOSH: Like fuck. *Papa?*

GEORGE: Odd. A man of that age. Status.

JOSH retrieves his water bottle.

To do with childhood. Breeding. Not the first time I've seen it. In the powerful. Some sense of shame. Beside a subordinate. In this case – you.

JOSH wrenches back the water bottle.

JOSH: Look, Sigmund fucking Freud: I don't know what's going on. But count yourself lucky. He's keeping you alive. Want to stay that way? Shut the fuck up. And don't give me any problems. We in the kill zone. If you must talk. Talk to him. Tell him anything.

BLACKOUT.

MARIMBA – TRAVELLING THEME.

SCENE SIX

<u>*The bush – now more dense*</u> – *its SOUNDS MORE DAUNTING. Spot on JOSH carrying GEORGE.*

JOSH: Christ, but you're heavy.

GEORGE: I didn't ask.

JOSH: For what?

GEORGE: To be carried.

JOSH: Doesn't make it easier.

GEORGE: You are not weak.

JOSH: *Fuck man, stop strangling me!*

    GEORGE adjusts his grip.

GEORGE: That better?

    They move.

JOSH: My heart's desire. Shlepping a bleeding gook through enemy bush.

GEORGE: Could be your deliverance. Vietcong, yes?

JOSH: Viet-what?

GEORGE: What they called them.

JOSH: Who?

GEORGE: The Yanks.

JOSH: Called what?

GEORGE: 'Gooks'.

JOSH: Don't give a toss.

GEORGE: A lot you don't seem to give a toss about, boy.

JOSH: Lugging you around, aren't I?

GEORGE: 'Gook.' – A term of insult.

JOSH: *Christ.*

GEORGE: Or…a sticky, wet mass.

JOSH: That's it. That's you. A wet…sticky…bloody mass.

    (Pause.)

GEORGE: How old are you?

JOSH: *Come on, man.*

GEORGE: Twenty? – You have an open face.

JOSH: Don't start, man.

GEORGE: What are you doing here? You're a long way from home.

JOSH: Dead right.

GEORGE: In a conscripted army.

JOSH: It was better than the alternative.

GEORGE: What was that?

JOSH: Jail. Jail or the army. That's the choice, wise guy.

GEORGE: So you chose this?

JOSH: *You try sharing a cell with a bunch of Jehovah's Witness!*

> *GEORGE laughs.*

PAPA: *(From a dark spot on the stage.)* Was it one of your jokes, Private?

JOSH: *JESUS!*

> *JOSH spins round instinctively pointing his rifle with his free hand. PAPA steps from the darkness.*

PAPA: Talking is he?

> *JOSH takes a moment to calm himself – on the point of hyperventilating.*

JOSH: No, sir. He just…laughed, man. From nowhere.

PAPA: He just…laughed. – Ja?

JOSH: That's right, sir.

PAPA: Then we must share the joke.

> *PAPA drags GEORGE off JOSH's back.*

GEORGE: Ovimbunyani…

PAPA: What?

> *PAPA pushes a boot into GEORGE's wound.*

Ovi-what?

GEORGE: *OVIMBUNYANI!*

PAPA: The man speaks. – *Progress.*

> *PAPA rolls the heel of his boot on GEORGE's wound. GEORGE screams.*

Not so funny now, is it?

> *PAPA shoves GEORGE away with his boot. GEORGE is wrenching in breath to control the pain.*

JOSH: *(Mouth dropping open.)* I…sorry… I…he…

PAPA: Does he seem like a FAPLA fighter? A SWAPO insurgent? A Cuban cadre? Use that posh education, mommy's boy. Could be the catch of a lifetime.

> *In the distance there is the RATTLE OF AN AK-47 MACHINE-GUN.*

Stay with him.

> *PAPA exits.*

GEORGE: *(In great pain.)* Jehovah's Witness…you say. They are denied heaven, you know. Doomed to tramp the earth until they convert another soul.

JOSH: Stop, man, please.

GEORGE: He's testing you.

JOSH: I'm asking you nicely.

GEORGE: It's part of his game.

JOSH: Don't talk to me any more!

GEORGE: Testing me.

JOSH: He'll do something to you.

GEORGE: We mustn't let him.

JOSH: Something bad.

GEORGE: Come sonny, talk to me!

JOSH: I said stop!

GEORGE: I must talk to *someone*!

JOSH: *Jesus!*

GEORGE: You have a choice here!

JOSH: I said I don't give a –.

GEORGE: *ARE YOU A MAN?*

> *BLACKOUT.*

> *MARIMBA – TRAVELLING THEME.*

SCENE SEVEN

The suggestion and SOUND OF A FAST FLOWING RIVER. JOSH freezes and stares ahead. He and GEORGE take in the scene.

GEORGE: Stunning. Isn't it? Our continent. The sudden changes. The majesty. Where life began, boy.

>   *(Pause.)*

GEORGE: This is a big occasion, Private. It shouldn't be wasted. Tell me about yourself.

JOSH: Why?

GEORGE: Because it's all I've got.

>   *There is MORTAR FIRE nearby. JOSH drops GEORGE. They hunker down.*

JOSH: *Where is he! Fuck!*

>   *JOSH punches his webbing in frustration, sucks in a few deep breaths, with it, the hint of hyperventilation, then he calms – and a short half-hysterical laugh bursts from him. He turns to look at GEORGE.*

GEORGE: *'If not now, when?'*

>   *(Beat.)*

We have been close, private. My blood on your back…piss.

JOSH: So?

GEORGE: *(In pain.)* Come…talk to me!

>   *JOSH turns away. MORTAR FIRE AGAIN, this time, further away.*

How old are you?

JOSH: *Not now, man.*

GEORGE: Twenty?

JOSH: Please…

GEORGE: You have an open face.

JOSH: *(Shutting his eyes.)* Stop.

GEORGE: You are from English stock. As far back as you know.

JOSH: *I said not now!*

GEORGE: Yes?

JOSH: *Yes!*

> *JOSH doesn't react, eyes still shut. There is a long silence, filled only by the sound of the RIVER.*

One Jewish granny.

GEORGE: Mazeltov.

> *(Pause.)*

JOSH: My ma's ma. *(Chuckling.)* Granny Lily.

GEORGE: Lily…?

JOSH: Dad's lot. They couldn't take her.

> *GEORGE waits…*

This crazy old creature, this alter Yiddisher lady. Swamped by WASPS. Know what she called them? The Gilmores? *'Vantzes'* Name for a bug. *(Perfect Lithuanian accent.)* 'Tvice I saw a vantz on de vall!'

> *GEORGE smiles.*

She wasn't like us. But she was okay. Only thing she passed on to yours truly? Fear of bugs, man! Can you believe it? Big blonde bastard like me.

GEORGE: You've been educated privately?

JOSH: My accent's a giveaway.

GEORGE: Things come easily to you…they always have…

JOSH: I've been lucky…

> *(Beat.)*

GEORGE: Your father…

> *JOSH looks away.*

…is stern? …devoted perhaps?

JOSH: We spend time together.

GEORGE: You close?

JOSH: He's my dad.

GEORGE: Are you close?

>*(Beat.)*

JOSH: He...trains me. Night and day. Since I was a kid. *(Sighing.) Since I was a kid...*

GEORGE: *(Delicately.)* You're an athlete.

JOSH: I run the hundred.

GEORGE: Are you fast?

JOSH: What's fast?

GEORGE: Nine point nine seconds?

JOSH: *(Laughing.)* That's the world record, dummy. – Ten point zero one.

>*GEORGE whistles.*

GEORGE: You're a champion.

JOSH: My dad, the top brass in the army, all of them, they all want me to do it. Crack ten.

GEORGE: Who's faster?

JOSH: In South Africa? Nobody.

GEORGE: Nobody white.

>*JOSH stares at him. The spell is broken. The light is fading fast. The sound of CICADAS intensifies.*

>*BLACKOUT.*

>*MARIMBA – TRAVELLING THEME.*

SCENE EIGHT

The bush. A dramatic sunset. GEORGE is slumped on JOSH's back, head resting on JOSH's shoulder. The effort of carrying GEORGE is now affecting JOSH gravely. He grimaces with each step. As he paces on he sings to himself to block out the pain.

JOSH: *Ma takes this badge off'a me...*

> *JOSH completes the first two lines of the first verse of 'Knockin'
> on Heaven's Door'.*

> *GEORGE's head is knocking on JOSH's shoulder.*

You kipping?

GEORGE: I was.

JOSH: Want to chat? So fucking chat.

GEORGE: When we move...like a knife... too much pain...

JOSH: I need something...anything...

GEORGE: What?

JOSH: *To take my mind off this!*

> *JOSH stops, on the point of hyperventilating. He drops to his
> knees with GEORGE on his back. He stares at the ground.*

Jesus, dear god...

> *GEORGE tries to dislodge himself.*

STAY ON!

> *JOSH battles to a standing position, hikes GEORGE up
> higher on his back, then resumes walking. JOSH tries to
> get back into a rhythm. He is struggling. They walk on.*

GEORGE: So. So. Then we talk. – Am I going to live?

JOSH: I don't know.

GEORGE: You can tell me.

JOSH: I'm not a medic.

GEORGE: You saw.

JOSH: If you get some help. If. You might. Are you South
African?

GEORGE: I can't answer that.

JOSH: Different rules, hey?

GEORGE: To protect you.

JOSH: Are you Zulu?

GEORGE: I can't answer that.

JOSH: What were you doing in that village? You 'can't answer that!'

GEORGE: Correct.

JOSH: Are you ANC?

GEORGE: You can have one more question.

JOSH: What do you want from me?

> *(Beat.)*

GEORGE: Morphine…

> *BLACKOUT.*

SCENE NINE

A derelict railway siding. Night. Suggestion of the hulk of an old steam train looming above, lying on its side. Moonlight bathes the place in a warm glow. JOSH, rifle across knees, sits, pensive. GEORGE is preoccupied, whittling away on a piece of wood with a stone.

JOSH: Sometimes… I think, this isn't happening. Not a dream. Something I can…*will away*. Before a race, I could see myself crossing the line. And I could also wipe it out. What I wanted, always happened.

> *(Pause.)*

I've been trapped with this tag. Since I was a tot. 'The blur.' Dad said I burst from ma's womb at full pelt. As a kid I was thrashing full-grown fuckers in the sprint. That kind of speed? Messes with people's heads. If I crack ten they'll dance in the streets. I'd be the quickest white man in the world. Now? When that day comes? I won't give a –

> *THREE SINGLE SHOTS in the distance then a FERAL SCREAM. GEORGE and JOSH stop, listen.*

JOSH: Papa…?

GEORGE: We live in hope.

> *JOSH laughs. GEORGE returns to the whittling. JOSH watches. GEORGE's concentration, despite his discomfort, is fierce.*

A soldier. Of wood. Wherever I go, I find timber…carve for my daughter. This one's special. He will salute.

JOSH: Your daughter?

> *GEORGE realises that he has let something slip and returns to the whittling. JOSH stays fixed on him.*

She have a name?

> *GEORGE hesitates—then seems to make a decision:*

GEORGE: Think of your insect lady…

JOSH: Lily!

> *GEORGE returns to whittling. JOSH unbuckles his knife and offers it to GEORGE.*

Finish it. Your toy.

> *GEORGE looks at the knife, then at JOSH, then smiles, acknowledging the display of trust. <u>PAPA appears, his hands smeared with blood.</u>*

Holy fuck.

> *JOSH's arm is still outstretched, offering the knife. He wrenches it back…but PAPA has registered the overt display of trust from JOSH.*

JOSH: How far are we from the border, sir?

PAPA: Twenty-five K.

> *PAPA strides over to GEORGE.*

Ovimbunyani, is it? Huh? 'Bloodsuckers'? That's what you think we are? Total onslaught from the communists through Africa and you people roll over and take it up the arse. We may have stumbled on a bigwig here, Private. One of our fellow countrymen skulking around the Angolan bush. Visiting SWAPO to suck up. A scorpion among snakes.

GEORGE: Ovimbunyani…

> *PAPA snaps a hand into GEORGE's groin.*

PAPA: Just one little ball left, my man… My man? Maybe not.

> *GEORGE reacts to the pressure but tries to hold on.*

Is it sore? Shame. Jusses. Feels it. Do you think you'll ever come again?

> *PAPA squeezes.*

GEORGE: *(Weakly.)* Badimo…

> *PAPA places his ear next to GEORGE's mouth.*

PAPA: Come again?

> *A stifled cry of pain in GEORGE's throat.*

Eina! Can you breathe? – Ja? Oh dear.

> *PAPA squeezes harder.*

Now while you can't. Ponder. I want to know things. I need facts. Pronto. How many of Mandela's scum are there in Angola? Huh?

> *PAPA applies maximum force.*

Jusses, I didn't know a ball could go that flat, my thumb is touching my forefinger.

> *JOSH turns away.*

YOU LOOK! You look here, Private!

> *JOSH turns slowly back. GEORGE looks at him, opens his mouth to speak, then passes out.*

PAPA: What did he say to you?

JOSH: I… I couldn't understand him.

PAPA: He was speaking Zulu?

JOSH: Can't be certain.

PAPA: Yet you offered him your knife?

JOSH: *Yes! I 'offered'! It's wood, sir!* Useless bloody… To carve some tiny, stupid… *The man's hardly going anywhere is he?* Christ! Not exactly Bruce fucking Lee.

> *(Beat.)*

PAPA: He's reeling you in like a fish.

JOSH stands to attention and salutes.

JOSH: Yes, Captain! Of course, Captain! No doubt, Captain! But who knows any more? And who gives a shit? *The point of the bloody exercise!*

JOSH is trembling, his jaw rigid with defiance. PAPA does not take his eyes off JOSH. Finally PAPA turns away from JOSH and starts to exit.

Off you trot then, sir. Next little jaunt is it?

PAPA stops and turns, slowly.

You were once in the Special Forces, am I right sir? A Colonel? Way back. – What happened?

PAPA is still as death.

I mean you're hardly a youngster – are you?

PAPA exits.

BLACKOUT.

SCENE TEN

<u>*Later. Early hours*</u>. *An unusual stillness. GEORGE is asleep. JOSH seems asleep. Beyond them PAPA stands on the siding, staring out, smoking. JOSH opens his eyes and watches PAPA. PAPA blows a smoke ring into the night air – it fades into the blackness. He chuckles, some thought engrossing him. He lets it ebb away.*

PAPA: Check it out, ma. Here I am, still watching trains.

He inclines his head in JOSH's direction.

Valhalla… You wouldn't know it. Farming town in the northern Cape. Place I grew up. – Perfect place.

He turns and looks directly at JOSH who at first turns away – then turns back. PAPA seems to reach a decision – and looks out at the night once again.

Autumn. Fifty-four. – The old steam train that ran between our village and Kimberly made its last journey. Everyone turned out to pay their respects – the whites, and the

Coloured workers from the farms. We stood on opposite
sides of the track. My ma beside me. The minutes came
and went. In silence.

(Pause.)

As the train passed a child stepped forward and…*saluted.* –
A gesture for us all. Then…*something happened. We cheered!*
Both sides of the track. Hats flew, people cried. There was
a kind of…*madness.* It was the death of something of what,
who can say? But it showed the heart of the place was
beating strong.

(Beat.)

That kid was me.

(Beat.)

Next morning my ma she complained of a headache. By
night she was dead. Thirty-one years old. Within a week I
was tramping the streets of Joburg with my pa. She'd been
a…a what?… Ja, let's say a…*significant figure* in both our
lives. He could not have continued to live in that village.

He was a…*sentimental man.* So he made a tactical choice.
And blew his brains out.

He turns and faces JOSH.

PAPA: And the only thing that rescued me in the next eight
years – years in which I also became a teenage father,
years I won't begin to describe to *you* – was – *the army.*
Because in it things were good again. Reconfirmed. Things
cut in stone from the day I was born. *And there, in that place,
as of old, in my uniform – I knew who I was.*

(Beat.)

What we are. What we will become. It's all here. In this
bush. In this war. *In me! In you! In him! THAT'S IT! THAT'S
ALL! AND THAT'S THE POINT OF THE FUCKING
EXERCISE!*

PAPA strides over to JOSH and wrenches him up.

Why didn't you want to do the officer's course?

JOSH: Jesus! What?

PAPA: You heard.

JOSH: Why you asking me that now, man!

PAPA: I've seen men beg for it. For a chance at serving their country.

JOSH: Well good fucking luck to them! Me? I want to see the world! Never want to carry a rifle again. And I didn't know how right I was. *Till now.*

PAPA: Pity.

> *PAPA releases JOSH.*

You would have made a good one.

JOSH: Like you.

PAPA: I'll say one thing. You've got balls.

> *He looks down at GEORGE.*

Unlike him.

> *BLACKOUT.*

> *MARIMBA TRAVELLING THEME.*

SCENE ELEVEN

The bush, southern Angola. Night. In the darkness, rain is falling from a blackened sky as GEORGE on JOSH's back, PAPA some way behind them, all covered in ponchos, walk across the landscape. Lights intensify and pick them up again at sunset:

GEORGE: We are melting, Private…into the night…into Africa…into each other…one life….one pain…one heart…

> *JOSH stops, releases GEORGE gently onto the ground. GEORGE appears to be unconscious. JOSH crawls into a foetal position. PAPA catches up, notes JOSH and GEORGE and squats down on his haunches. He senses something, sniffs the air. A moment's silence, then:*

The beautiful sound of a WOMAN's VOICE SINGING 'Angola Avante' (The Angolan national anthem) reaches them, floating across the bush.

WOMAN: *(Offstage.)* ... Honramos o passado e a nossa História,

Construindo no Trabalho o Homem novo,

JOSH sits up and smiles broadly.

JOSH: Wow!

WOMAN: *(Offstage.)*
... Angola, avante! Revolução, pelo Poder Popular!
Pátria Unida, Liberdade,
Um só povo, uma só Nação

JOSH: Just listen to that, sir!

PAPA's face is like stone. His eyes stay locked on JOSH. JOSH's elation quickly evaporates. JOSH refuses to look away.

(Softly.) Why?

The stillness in PAPA is complete, eyes dark, disclosing nothing. A young WAMBO WOMAN, her hair in beads, in a brightly coloured skirt and with a BABY strapped to her back, appears.

WOMAN: *Angola, avante! Revolução, pelo Poder Popu* –

She stops dead when she sees them, the song dying in her throat. Her lip trembles but she tries to stay calm.

PAPA: *(Softly.)* A country of women.

WOMAN: I...walk home.

PAPA: Where?

WOMAN: Caluenha...

PAPA studies her. She plucks up courage and slowly, she smiles.

PAPA: See Private? She's also going home.

PAPA smiles back at her.

Many SWAPO there, huh?

WOMAN: Too much killing.

> *PAPA nods. The WOMAN is uncertain. PAPA gestures grandly for her to go on her way. She hesitates – smiles coyly at JOSH who smiles back.*

Obrigado…

> *She continues to walk on her way. JOSH stares at her. Her eyes are now averted as she passes. PAPA watches her receding figure, the baby with its lolling head.*

PAPA: Missus…

> *She continues. PAPA whistles. She stops. PAPA turns to JOSH.*

Learn.

> *PAPA walks to the WOMAN. He stops beside her and opens his arms.*

Baba…

> *She remains still.*

Baba!

> *She starts to tremble. PAPA roughly undoes the blanket holding the baby. It flops out into his arms.*

JOSH: *No, sir…!*

> *JOSH looks down at the baby – his face registering shock. PAPA lays it gently on the ground. It is dead. He rolls back the swaddling.*

PAPA: These fucking people.

> *Running from stomach to neck are crude stitches.*

JOSH: *Aoooww – Jesus, man! – WHY?*

> *JOSH turns to the WOMAN who is now terror-stricken. PAPA takes out his survival knife.*

Oh, man, what the fuck you –

> *JOSH turns away, hyperventilating, eyes mad, then squats, hands over his face, as PAPA gets to work, slicing open the stitches.*

No man–no man–no man–no man–no man–no man–no man–

> *PAPA stands. In his hand is a cloth sack, removed from the baby. He upends the sack – grenades drop out on to the ground.*

NOOOOOOOOO!

> *PAPA points his pistol at the WOMAN.*

PAPA: Here, there is no 'why.'

> *BLACKOUT.*

SCENE TWELVE

<u>*Suggestion of a shack*</u> *– dusk. JOSH, GEORGE on his back, utterly done in, staggers towards a corrugated shack in a clearing. JOSH lets out a cry of pain, collapses, lets GEORGE tumble heavily. JOSH crawls into a foetal position. PAPA enters and watches JOSH, concerned. He goes to him. The light is fading fast.*

PAPA: Gilmore.

> *PAPA prods him. JOSH's eyes half open – he is delirious.* <u>*PAPA reaches out… JOSH starts to hyperventilate. PAPA retracts his hand*</u>*. GEORGE watches them. PAPA takes a bar of chocolate from his webbing and offers it to JOSH who eyes it suspiciously, then grabs the chocolate and wolfs it down.*

Gilmore…you on night patrol. Take a break.

> *Revived by the food, JOSH stands, takes his rifle and moves offstage. PAPA and GEORGE are alone. PAPA watches him. GEORGE refuses eye contact. PAPA offers GEORGE a cigarette. GEORGE is impassive.*

Just a fucking cigarette.

> *GEORGE extends his hand, palm upwards. PAPA drops the cigarette into it, throws him a pack of matches. GEORGE lights up. Heaven. Their faces are illuminated by the glow of the cigarette.*

This thing of silence. I respect that. You and me. We know what's worth dying for. As for the boy. Forget it. Gives a shit about nothing. Except himself.

>*PAPA stands and walks over, sits beside GEORGE.*
>*GEORGE shudders.*

Got you down as a politico. Not a full-time soldier. Hands too soft. Eyes too shifty. Makes you precious. I got to do this. Get it out of you.

>*PAPA produces a syringe from his pocket.*

Found this. Penicillin. When I took off the heads of your comrades.

>*GEORGE's face contorts in disgust.*

One shot'll do the trick. Stop that gangrene.

>*He brings the syringe closer to GEORGE's arm.*

Save your leg.

>*He flicks the syringe with a finger to rid it of bubbles.*

PAPA: Life.

>*PAPA brings the syringe close to GEORGE's arm.*

>*GEORGE is silent, eyes burning into PAPA.*

The steady gaze of the Judas.

>*PAPA starts to squirt out the contents of the syringe.*
>*JOSH enters unseen.*

JOSH: *Sir!*

>*PAPA wheels round, pistol pointed as JOSH enters.*

PAPA: Never do that again.

JOSH: Sorry, sir.

>*PAPA looks at the syringe – there is some liquid left. He pushes slowly, making it dribble out, eyes on GEORGE.*

Wait!

>*JOSH squats beside PAPA. GEORGE's eyes are burning into JOSH.*

No fucking good to us dead, is he sir?

>*PAPA stares at him.*

Got this far! Let's haul him back, sir! *The treacherous terr bastard!*

> *JOSH reaches for the syringe.*

Find out what's in that 'nasty black mind'.

> *(Beat.)*

PAPA: Be very sure of what you're doing.

> *PAPA allows JOSH to take the syringe and exits. JOSH holds the syringe to the light. There is some liquid left. JOSH injects GEORGE. JOSH, energised, stands, sheds some pack, readjusts his webbing and swivels his kidney pouches onto either hip. JOSH is ready. He goes to GEORGE, hauls him to a standing position. JOSH slaps his kidney pouches now on either hip.*

JOSH: Mount up Tonto.

> *He hauls GEORGE onto his back. GEORGE places the front of his ankles on top of the pouches, so he is perched like a jockey.*

Wait.

> *JOSH takes a short section of rope from a pouch, flips it over his head and straps GEORGE to his back. JOSH tests the new arrangement, shaking GEORGE, then satisfied, moves off.*

GEORGE: Thank you.

JOSH: We're returning to plan A.

GEORGE: And what's that?

JOSH: *Shut the fuck up.*

> *BLACKOUT.*

> *MARIMBA – TRAVELLING THEME.*

SCENE THIRTEEN

JOSH and GEORGE move through the bush. The lighting goes through several dazzling changes, indicating different terrain and moving through night and back to day, until there is the suggestion of a sandy plain. MORTARS sound from some distance away…

PAPA: *(From the darkness.)* DOWN!

The lights snap on: it is dusk. JOSH runs towards shelter GEORGE on his back, PAPA following, as MORTARS begin to land around them…

Cover!

PAPA dives down. JOSH lets GEORGE flop onto the ground and both men flatten themselves. The pounding continues for a moment – then stops.

JOSH: *JESUS! JESUS CHRIST! FUCKING ANTS!* This is the end, man!

JOSH slaps at his body, crazed, running out into the open.

SHIT! SHIT!

PAPA: Stay where you were, Private!

WOMP! WOMP! – shells land.

JOSH: *Let them bomb me! Better than these little red bastards!*

PAPA jumps from the mound as MORTARS continue to fall round them. He hauls JOSH back to cover as JOSH struggles, brushing violently at his body.

Aaaah! Aaaah!…

PAPA wrenches him up. JOSH stares up at PAPA wide-eyed, body wracked.

PAPA: The enemy's getting desperate. They'd rather have him dead than in our hands. *You made a strong choice, Private. A brave choice!*

PAPA sprints off. JOSH continues to brush off the ants.

JOSH: Jesus, get off me! *Bloody vantzes!*

Suddenly there is a new sound amidst the screaming and bombs – laughter – erupting from GEORGE as he watches JOSH continue his Dervish-like dance. The MORTARS stop. JOSH breathes heavily, and outraged, glares at GEORGE.

(A pathetic squeak.) My body's on fire, man!

He realises that there are ants crawling over GEORGE.

Shame man! Sorry, man!

He brushes the ants off GEORGE's body.

GEORGE: *(Weakly.)* I got one ball and gangrene, and my comrades want to kill me, what's a few fucking ants?

> *JOSH suddenly seems to see the humour − but there is something out of joint in his laughter. JOSH bends down over GEORGE − who suddenly appears to be lifeless − and shouts directly into his face, laughter unabated.*

JOSH: *Why we being routed? They told us we could reach Cairo without a scratch. Hey?*

> *He lifts GEORGE up by the lapels − shakes him.*

Hey?

> *The shaking becomes more violent.*

(Laughter increasing.) Hey-hey? *Babies? No bowels in BABIES! I mean − what − the − fuck − is − that? DEAD − FUCKING − BABY − FUCKING − BOMB?! Hey!? (Starts to hyperventilate.) Hey-hey-hey-hey-hey-hey!?*

GEORGE: People who come to that. Such people. Can never be beaten.

> *JOSH's breaths are now rasping, tearing at him.*

Breathe into your jacket.

JOSH: *Huh? Wha…?*

GEORGE: You're going to faint if you do that. Breathe into your jacket.

> *JOSH buries his face in his bush-jacket.*

Take in your own carbon-dioxide. Too much oxygen…in your blood.

> *Slowly, JOSH begins to calm down.*

JOSH: *(Between breaths.)* I thought you were dead! Why's he doing this? *WHY'S HE DOING THIS?* My legs! The bones are split apart? I can't carry you another inch. I can't go on. I just can't man.

GEORGE: *(In pain.)* You know you can.

PAPA: *(Offstage.) MOVE OUT!*

> *JOSH goes to GEORGE, kneels. GEORGE, with great difficulty, drags himself onto JOSH's back. JOSH grimaces in pain. GEORGE lays his head on JOSH's shoulder. MARIMBA: TRAVELLING THEME. <u>Lights dim, isolating JOSH and GEORGE.</u>*

JOSH: Daddy help me… *Help me DADDY!*

> *JOSH wrenches himself and GEORGE up. He staggers slowly forward.*

Nothing left…no blood in my heart…nothing… *'Easy in the blocks…stare down the barrel…break the tape in your mind…relax for the bang…let it release you…wait…wait…'*

> *SHELLING, MACHINE-GUN FIRE starts and continues. JOSH and GEORGE stagger together, silhouetted by the flashes.*
>
> *BLACKOUT.*

SCENE FOURTEEN

<u>A mountain slope</u>. Dawn. JOSH lets GEORGE slide to the ground. JOSH cradles him like a child, takes a flask from his hip pocket.

JOSH: Here. Pineapple beer. My own brew.

> *GEORGE toasts JOSH.*

GEORGE: Aluta Continua.

JOSH: Come again?

GEORGE: 'The struggle continues.'

JOSH: Only one arsehole struggling around here, man – me.

> *GEORGE smiles then drinks, not stopping.*

Hey!

> *JOSH laughs, takes the flask and drinks.*

Remember how Sinbad got the old man off his back? First got him drunk.

> *GEORGE laughs – JOSH joins in. There is now an ease – an intimacy between them.*

JOSH: Till now, know what scared me most? Not pleasing my dad. Hope I live long enough to be drunk again. Have one last fuck.

GEORGE: Can't help you.

JOSH: Hey?

GEORGE: Immorality act.

JOSH: *(Laughing.)* Watch it.

> *(Beat.)*

Out here? No doubters. When you scared, you find god.

> *GEORGE shuts his eyes as a spasm of pain grips him. He digs deep.*

GEORGE: We turn elsewhere.

> *JOSH sees that GEORGE is trying to stay conscious.*

JOSH: *(Quickly.)* Who?

GEORGE: Africans.

JOSH: Where?

GEORGE: To our ancestors.

> *MARIMBA…*

In times of joy…sorrow…it's to them we turn for… intercession.

> *JOSH shakes him.*

JOSH: For what?

GEORGE: Judgment…final judgment.

JOSH: And you…?

GEORGE: Even an old atheist like me – I still believe in their power.

> *(Pause.)*

You have a grandfather?

> *JOSH nods.*

GEORGE: Uncles? Aunts? Loved ones who have passed away?

JOSH nods.

Going back for centuries…thousands upon thousands of Gilmores.

JOSH laughs. GEORGE's eyes grow heavy.

(Almost a whisper.) Ever talk to them?

JOSH considers this for a moment, shakes his head. He tries to shift position.

JOSH: Shit… I'll never get up again.

JOSH sees GEORGE is unconscious. Instinctively, he pulls GEORGE closer. He studies GEORGE's face keeping him cradled in his arms.

Don't die now, man, don't you dare fucking die you old bastard.

PAPA steps in from the bush, taking in the scene. JOSH makes no effort to hide the intimacy.

PAPA: What you doing, Private? Maybe it's time to let me carry him.

JOSH: NO!

PAPA stares at him.

No, sir. I… I'm alright. Used to it. I'm still strong.

PAPA: Good. They said you could run like the wind. And now that's what you're going to have to do. Reinforced FAPLA columns coming at us from the north. West, a unit of Cubans.

JOSH: We've had it.

PAPA: *(With inexplicable tenderness.)* Never say die, boetie. Okay?

JOSH: Ja. Okay.

PAPA: There's a way. We sneak through the last stretch to the border by night.

JOSH: The whole army's retreating, isn't it?

PAPA freezes. GEORGE opens his eyes, suddenly alert. PAPA notices. GEORGE shuts his eyes again... PAPA chuckles to himself.

PAPA: Yes, Private.

PAPA squats down and shoves his face close to GEORGE.

The whole army's retreating. *(Smiles at GEORGE.)* Move him to the ridge.

PAPA exits into the bush.

GEORGE: Now he has an excuse to kill me. I know too much.

JOSH: He won't kill you. You're important.

GEORGE: He thinks I'm some general.

JOSH: Are you?

GEORGE huriedly reaches inside his bloodied shirt, removes the WOODEN SOLDIER, holds it to the light: it is crude, but full of life, a hunched little cedar man, arm raised in salute.

GEORGE: Here's the general...just in time.

JOSH: Shit, that's good!

GEORGE stands. JOSH stares up at him, mouth open.

How the fuck did you manage that?

GEORGE: Years of whittling in cold corridors, I –

GEORGE realises that he has managed to stand unaided. JOSH applauds. GEORGE bows, then grimaces in pain, laughs, and sinks back to the ground.

JOSH: You going to make it...

JOSH points towards the bush.

Beyond that... Heaven's door...home.

GEORGE smiles weakly. JOSH comes to him, stretches out a hand. GEORGE takes it.

GEORGE: St. Christopher or Sinbad...?

The two men scream in pain as JOSH hauls GEORGE to his feet. GEORGE settles on JOSH's back.

> *MARIMBA, TRAVELLING THEME. <u>The lights change as they move into the bush.</u>*

JOSH: …knock knock knockin' on heaven's door…

GEORGE: Second verse…

JOSH: Aaah, no, man.

GEORGE: There's only one?

JOSH: Can't remember.

GEORGE: Try…

> *(Beat.)*

JOSH: *(Pause.) Ma put…wait…ja…'ma put my guns in the ground…*

> *JOSH completes the second verse of 'Knockin' on Heaven's Door' ending on –*

Feel like I'm...'

GEORGE: 'Knockin' on heaven's door'?

> *JOSH and GEORGE sing the first two lines of the chorus together.*
>
> *They laugh as the lights dissolve quickly into:*

SCENE FIFTEEN

<u>*Suggestion of a waterfall*</u>*. Naulila falls. Day. In the distance there is the sound of a WATERFALL. JOSH enters, carrying GEORGE. JOSH's knees suddenly buckle. He collapses forward with GEORGE strapped to his back. GEORGE lies on top of him. Neither man moves for several seconds.*

GEORGE: I know a joke.

JOSH: Uh-huh?

GEORGE: I think you'll like it.

JOSH: Shoot.

> *(Beat.)*

GEORGE: Mr and Mrs Kaplan both in their eighties, go to the doctor. The doctor says: *'I've got the results of your blood test Mr. Kaplan – and I'm afraid you have a terminal disease.'* They stare at him, shocked. *'However'* says the doctor, *'There is one cure. But before I reveal it I'd like Mr. Kaplan to leave the room.'* Alone with Mrs. Kaplan the doctor says, *'The only thing that can cure your husband – is oral sex.'* Mrs. Kaplan thanks the doctor and finds Mr. Kaplan in the waiting room. – *'Hymie'* she says, *'You're going to die.'*

> *JOSH chuckles – and they set each other off, the laughter cascading out of them. <u>There is a sudden salvo of unearthly sonic BOOMS followed by a series of MASSIVE EXPLOSIONS.</u> JOSH rolls over onto his side taking GEORGE with him.*

JOSH: *What the fuck was that?*

GEORGE: The 'Red Eye.'

JOSH: The what?

GEORGE: Stalin organ rocket launcher.

JOSH: Hey?

GEORGE: It's them. *The Cubanos! Thousands of them. Pushing ever south.*

> *JOSH unties the binding rope at speed.*

And when your army's retreat is over, it will be the turning point. Because it will show us you can be beaten.

JOSH: It's not my war.

> *GEORGE, now freed, grabs JOSH by his lapels.*

GEORGE: *DO YOU KNOW WHAT YOUR COUNTRY HAS DONE? DO YOU?*

> *JOSH stares at him, open-mouthed.*

GEORGE: Every country in the world knows the South African army's in Angola. Except one. *South Africa.* You're not meant to be here. And if you die in this place, your family will be told lies. Keeping you in ignorance. That's the secret weapon of your republic.

JOSH: Listen, old man. Don't lecture me, OK? You think you're a saint?

GEORGE: I stabbed a man in the throat with a bicycle spoke when I was eighteen and I watched as the blood bubbled up through the hole. I took all his money and gave nothing to my dying father. I was married to the same woman for twenty years but I've loved many. I have children I've never met and my daughter's spent three months with me in ten years. I'm a sinner, Private. And fate's been wicked. *I got you for my last confession.*

  (Beat.)

JOSH: Did the man die?

GEORGE: I don't know.

JOSH: What happened to you?

GEORGE: They sent me to prison. To Robben Island. *And that's when I started to learn.*

  (Beat.)

I should not have berated you. Few men could have done what you did in the last five days.

JOSH: Forget it.

GEORGE: It's…the pain. I fear… I'll talk.

  JOSH rips off his webbing and gives it to GEORGE as a pillow. GEORGE rests his head on it.

JOSH: Then make something up. Tell him anything. It's not his job to interrogate you. The sick fuck!

  PAPA appears and listens, unseen, from the bush.

GEORGE: I won't forget you, Private. You…have something in you.

JOSH: Josh…my name is Josh.

GEORGE: 'Saviour.' It's meaning. Did you know?

  JOSH searches GEORGE's face.

JOSH: You talk, but you don't tell.

  (Pause)

He's tortured me too. Why should I fucking tell him anything! Papa might be bushfucked but he's a clever bastard. And I think you are a general, an important man. So why don't you tell me the truth?

GEORGE: For you...for others, I cannot. So...for the moment...*you tell me yours.*

JOSH: This. Now. That's all I know. This and you. A year ago I'm a national hero. Six months ago I pledge my silence to the army to the grave. A week later I sign some affidavit to say I'm not a fucking South African. We hide in a hangar in Libito to avoid the foreign press. We burn every pathetic Wambo village we go through. My C.O's trying to break me. I've become the friend of a black terrorist. So you tell me what the damn truth is! *YOU TELL ME!*

> *GEORGE looks at JOSH – long and hard.*

GEORGE: You want the truth? Then let me give you the biggest truth there is. Think you can take it, boy?

> *(Beat.)*

There are talks going on. Big talks. Between important people. Talks few people know about. Things are about to change in our country. And we will become the focus of the world.

JOSH: Change?

> *(Beat.)*

GEORGE: The release of Nelson Mandela.

JOSH: Holy fuck.

GEORGE: And from that day forth your racist republic will start to die.

PAPA: *Ovimbunyani...*

> *JOSH spins round and sees PAPA. PAPA is dead still. JOSH starts to shake.*

JOSH: Sir...sir, I...

> *PAPA walks slowly up to JOSH.*

PAPA: Did you fuck him, Private? 'Cause he's certainly fucked you.

JOSH: Sir, he's told me nothing, sir. He just…talks kak from morning to night.

PAPA: And there's no kak…quite like kaffir kak, is there?

> *(Pause.)*

If we don't make the Okavango by dawn, we're dead. That's the bad news. *(Smiles.)* I can see you're just… dying to know the good. You're going solo again, Private. Without this…

> *He pushes GEORGE over with his foot.*

…fetid black lump clinging to your neck, we should make it home. And when we get there…you can say you've done something for your country.

> *PAPA removes his pistol from its holster and holds it out to JOSH.*

Take the pistol, Private.

> *JOSH stares at it. His jaw drops.*

Take it.

JOSH: It's…not my weapon…sir.

PAPA: I know that.

> *JOSH obeys, wide-eyed.*

It makes less noise.

JOSH: Hey?… And now? What…what do I –

PAPA: Wait till there's gunfire. Then…proceed.

JOSH: With what…?

> *PAPA's face is like stone.*

Don't…do this, sir.

PAPA: Put it against his head and pull the trigger.

> *JOSH looks down. He opens his mouth to speak. No sound comes.*

PAPA: It's a gift...from me...to you.

JOSH: No, man. No way, man.

PAPA: It's an order.

JOSH: *YOU!* –– why? –– *It's madness.*

PAPA: It's war. Do it, there's glory. The man's a high-ranking ANC operative. A bush execution's too good for him.

JOSH: He...please... I... I'm not the one to...not me...

PAPA is motionless.

YOU CAN'T DO THIS, MAN! HOW CAN YOU DO THIS?

PAPA: Disobey me and I'll inform the Ministry Of Defence, I'll tell the President himself, how you fraternised, how you grovelled – how you slept with the enemy. That has an end: *you will have run your last fucking race.* – I'll give you a minute. Or – when I get back– I'll do it myself.

PAPA exits. JOSH buries his face in his hands.

JOSH: *This is hell, Christ, this is...hell!*

GEORGE: This is what he wanted.

JOSH: Why?

GEORGE: He's in his own hell. He just wants to bring you to it.

JOSH: What does that mean?

GEORGE reaches over and pulls JOSH to him.

GEORGE: Listen to me. If... I get back, I face torture, maybe worse... *Rather you...than him...*

(Beat.)

Live, for me.

JOSH: Why's it happening? Why's this happening?

GEORGE: No other man could have done what you did. *Look at me!* Many have died to bring about change. People like you must defend that hard-won freedom. So our leaders never again betray their own people.

JOSH: Jesus, oh, dear Jesus...

GEORGE hands the WOODEN SOLDIER to JOSH.

GEORGE: Take this. *(Softly.)* Isi khumbuso. It's a… remembrance. Give it to Lily, my daughter. From it, she'll know me. She lives in London with her aunt.

JOSH: London?

GEORGE: You'll find her. Will you do this for me?

JOSH takes the carving. He stares at it.

Promise me.

JOSH pockets the carving.

JOSH: I…promise.

GEORGE: Tell her, my…family, how I went. And…please… this place, this…spot, fix it in your memory. They will want to know.

JOSH: Sweet Jesus… Sweet Jesus…

A SHORT BURST OF MACHINE-GUN FIRE.

JOSH closes his eyes.

GEORGE: This. All of this, has been for a reason.

JOSH: *For bullshit, that's what it's been for!*

GEORGE: It can only have meaning…if you know why it came to pass. Now…find strength in your heart.

JOSH: Aaaah…no, man, I… *(A howl.) NOOOO! Jesus, Daddy, help meeeee…!*

GEORGE: Take my hand.

JOSH extends a hand to GEORGE. GEORGE stretches out his. They clasp. Slowly, JOSH's breathing settles.

JOSH: I don't know your name.

(Pause.)

GEORGE: Jozana. George… Jozana.

A BURST OF MACHINE-GUN FIRE in the distance. GEORGE and JOSH stay motionless, locked together.

Slowly, JOSH moves round the back of GEORGE, keeping hold of his hand. They take a tighter grip on each other, almost an embrace.

JOSH puts the pistol to the back of GEORGE's head.

GEORGE: I am not so brave…after all. Sing to me.

(Pause.)

JOSH sings the third line of the second verse of 'Knockin' on Heaven's Door'.

GEORGE: Sing!

JOSH: Feel like I'm…

GEORGE: *SING, WHITE BOY!*

JOSH: *Knockin' on Heaven's Door,*
knock knock knockin' on…
– oh Jesus…

THE MACHINE-GUN FIRE stops. Silence.

… Forgive me…

JOSH's lips move silently.

THE MACHINE –GUN FIRE starts up again.

Now.

GEORGE: *Abakhulu Baka Jozana!*

GUNSHOT / BLACKOUT.

ACT THREE

SCENE ONE

A graveside. Cape Town. The present. JOSH and LILY face one another. JOSH is in his late 30s. LILY is still, her eyes on him. GEORGE appears from the darkness, takes in the situation, looking longingly at LILY, who has no awareness of his presence.

JOSH: *(To LILY.)* I've…always known where you were. I kept track of you. We lived near each other in London for many years. When you finally returned so long after the elections, it felt very strange.

> *She remains still.*

I know…it must be the hardest thing you've ever done, listening to that story. I tried to explain…cover as much as I could. I'm sure I failed. But then my life…

> *She does not respond. JOSH starts to hyperventilate.*

GEORGE: *(To JOSH.)* Breathe into your jacket…

> *He breathes into his jacket and starts to calm down.*

JOSH: I was acting under orders. That's not an excuse. I simply didn't have the courage to disobey. I'm not asking for forgiveness. How could you grant it? All I can do is express my remorse, my sorrow and…*shame* for what happened to your father – *Jesus, how useless is language* – and offer an… apology for what I did.

> *(Pause.)*

LILY: A what?

JOSH: I / want to –

LILY: /You're trying to do what?

JOSH: Please, I…

LILY: You talk of courage…? Twenty years? *Twenty years!*

JOSH: I know / it must –

LILY: / You knew where I lived. You say you sought me out. I was ten when he died now I'm thirty. What were you doing? *Running? Hiding? Spying!* To what end? You say you felt strange when I returned. To know that I did you must have tracked my movements. And for what? For who? *For the right time, Mr. Gilmore, the right time for you.* What do you want?

JOSH: Some kind of...justice.

LILY: *For who?*

JOSH: A month after it happened the war ended. And Papa Louw vanished. If I find him there may be little that can be done officially as the crime was committed on foreign soil. And of course the truth commission no longer exists. And the country no longer seems to have the appetite. *But I intend to force him out from under his rock.*

LILY: I see. And this is for me? For my father? The country? You purge yourself and your colleague walks free. What is that?

JOSH: If *that* happens... I have other plans.

LILY: *You people...never change!* Even now you still think you have some god-given authority. You do not...have the right – to do anything that affects me. You know nothing about me.

JOSH: I know that he loved you.

LILY: *You are not the person to tell me!*

JOSH: I owe him. I owe your father. He wouldn't have wanted this. Wanted nothing.

LILY: He wouldn't. But he's dead.

JOSH: Then what? What do you want of me? What do I do?

LILY: You walk the streets a free man. Failure is a luxury. You stand here, alive, in good clothes, and say you're sorry for butchering my father. Twenty years too late! I didn't come to hear that.

> *She moves off.*

JOSH: Why did you come?

She stops and turns.

LILY: The why is easy. The pain of the families of the dead is *not knowing*. How. When. Where.

(Beat.)

I came for the Jozanas. We are a large family, Mr. Gilmore. And it is to us, all of us, that you must answer.

(Pause.)

JOSH: Sixty kilometres north of Ondangwa on the Namibian border are the Naulila Falls. If you stand with your back to them, facing north, you'll see a hillock sticking out of the earth, about the height of a man.

(Pause.)

I shot your father at the base of that hillock.

(Pause.)

LILY: Thank you.

(Pause.)

Many years have passed, Mr. Gilmore. New hillocks will have formed, old ones, gone. The spot. The…exact spot. Would you know it?

He nods, bracing himself –

Show me

The impulse to hyperventilate overtakes him and he turns away.

Please…

ECHOING GUNSHOT – JOSH claps his hands to his ears. LILY is motionless, watching him. Slowly, his hands drop.

JOSH: Anything else. Not that. Don't ask me for that.

BLACKOUT.

SCENE TWO

<u>A night watchman's railway shed in Cape Town</u>. The present. Notices in Xhosa, Afrikaans and English adorn the walls. In the centre of the room is a table and chair. On the table are books and a hipflask. Slumped on the table is a man. A lamp above his head illuminates the shed in a dim light. JOSH, briefcase in hand, is watching the man. A TRAIN APPROACHES in the distance.

JOSH: Papa…?

MAN: *(Not looking up.)* Huh?

JOSH: I'm looking for…

> *The man – PAPA – looks up, sees JOSH and chuckles. PAPA has aged considerably. He is dishevelled and appears slightly inebriated.*

Captain?

PAPA: Not a pretty sight, is it?

> *(Beat.)*

Hello… Private.

JOSH: *You?*

PAPA: Ja. You should knock. Lucky I didn't shoot you.

> *PAPA pours a drink from his hipflask.*

Last week my colleague had his fingers chopped off by an intruder. Who let you in the gate?

JOSH: A man with no fingers.

PAPA: Still the clown.

JOSH: Wait and see.

> *PAPA drinks. JOSH watches him.*

PAPA: How'd you get this address?

JOSH: Your wife.

PAPA: She loves charity.

> *The TRAIN SHUNTS past, its light strobing the shed <u>revealing GEORGE in a corner, watching, dead still</u>.*

81

They're closing this line next month. Oldest shunting yard in Africa. It was once connected to the docks. All sorts of stuff came through here. Spices. Cloth. You name it. Now it's Nintendo from Thailand. Kindles from Ukraine and porno from Peru. Times have changed.

JOSH: Have you?

> *JOSH reaches for his briefcase.*

PAPA: Stop.

> *PAPA pulls a pistol from his pocket.*

JOSH: What you afraid of?

PAPA: The Lone Ranger.

> *(Pause.)*

Empty it on the desk.

> *JOSH empties the briefcase: three bound files drop out. PAPA examines their titles one by one.*

'Latvian collusion in the holocaust; Serbian genocide in the Balkans; South African atrocities in the Angolan war: A Truth Commission Report.'

> *PAPA lifts the last file. It is flimsy. He smiles, drops it on the desk.*

JOSH: Has an odd ring. I don't think the truth *can* be commissioned. It's like forcing a vulture to puke up its prey.

PAPA: This for me? I like a good read.

> *PAPA places the pistol on the desk.*

'Incongruous.'

JOSH: What?

PAPA: It's better than 'odd.' You said 'odd.' That it has an 'odd ring.' Isn't it a pleasure to describe something in a way that explains exactly what it is? You pulled me up once. Something to do with the senses. The difference between smell and aroma. Remember?

JOSH: I remember.

PAPA: Maybe that's why I'm obsessed with time. And statistics. A sort of thin replacement of my inner-need for eloquence. Shit, that was unexpected! – A revelation at two in the morning.

JOSH: I remember every detail from the day we met.

PAPA: I'm touched. *(Referring to books.)* Marx, Huxley… Hitchens. When *we* knew each other it was strictly Batman and Robin. But now I *devour* good works. And with time on my hands, I can make up for the loss of it.

JOSH: Your voice…little ways. Never left me. Sometimes, in company, in the middle of conversation, *there you were.*

PAPA: Conversation, hey? How I long for it. Most of my friends vanished when my shop folded up. It was amazing. The speed of it. One moment I was making a living then zap, round the millennium, people stopped buying my goods. From one day to the next.

JOSH: I've relived Angola many times. But there are ten minutes in particular… I go over…again…and again / and again.

PAPA: / My wife and son, they… *Stood by me…*for a while. We sold everything we had. Including our home. To foreigners. A young… *Oriental couple* who used it for holidays. It was round then I hit the J&B. She told me if I didn't pull myself together and find work I could go. And after a year, a year of hell, I did. To the only place that would take me: an emergency caravan site for poor whites. Thirty years of marriage. Phut. Gone. Because there was nothing. Nothing left for a pissed, penniless Boer in the new South Africa. Except one task. – *Reflection…*

> *PAPA toasts JOSH with his hipflask.*

JOSH: *SHUT YOUR FACE!*

> *JOSH hits the flask from PAPA's hand. It smashes against the wall. A TRAIN SHUNTS BY, TOOTING in the night. Silence…*

> *Someone BANGS LOUDLY THREE TIMES ON THE SHED and shouts in Xhosa:*

SIGNALMAN: *(Offstage.) Isitimela se ku gcina siyeza!*

PAPA: *Ewe!*… My colleague…the last train is coming.

> *PAPA gets up and retrieves the hipflask.*

Please…don't ever repeat…what you just did.

> *PAPA moves back to the table.*

And now, maybe, you should spit it out.

JOSH: You know why I'm back. Why I'm here. I didn't come to hear you bleat.

PAPA: What *did* you come for?

JOSH: An ending.

> *(Beat.)*

Judgment.

> *(Beat.)*

Justice.

> *(Beat.)*

PAPA: Valhalla…

JOSH: What?

PAPA: You wouldn't know it. A farming town in the Cape. It's the place I grew up. A perfect place. But then…my *ma* died…when I was nine / and we

JOSH: */ I know that epic.*

PAPA: *(Rising.) You barge in here after twenty years with your burning torch, meneer. You want to debate with me? Then listen or fade away!*

> *(Pause.)*

You caught me at a bad time. Justice, hey?

> *(Pause.)*

Nothing…

84

PAPA clutches his head and smashes the table three times – it seems to settle him.

PAPA: There was nothing that stood between me and what I wanted there on the farm before we moved before she died it was all there you can never prove it was any other way because I was there. And I remember… It was unequal. What thing of beauty is ever not?

>   *(Beat.)*

Since then the earth has shifted.

>   *(Beat.)*

I sit here at the age of sixty-five, watching trains. In a land of broken promises. I've lost my family and my job. My boss is black as night. And I'm still bushfucked after all these years. *But I'm alive!* And it's taken me a while. But I'm not who I was. The mistake you English made was to paint us as dumb. The truth is a gulf away. We did things the way we wanted for three centuries and when the time came we had the guile to change. We defied the world, we denied the left their day of reckoning. And that's what sticks in your craw: *We're here! We're still alive! And in the end we didn't get a hiding.* You think you can scare me? After what I've been through? You think you smell of roses? *IT WAS A FUCKING WAR, YOU FUCKING FRAUD. WHAT DO YOU THINK IT WAS?* I did what I did in the bush and I had to do it. And no judge, no man, no god is going to find otherwise: in camera, off camera, or at the end of a fucking rope!

PAPA takes a drink and sits back, exhausted.

JOSH: Not a night has passed…without the same image in my mind…your head…exploding like a melon. Like Jozana's. And no matter how often that image returns I hear this voice, saying the same thing over and over and over – 'A gift from me to you.' That voice is yours.

>   *(Beat.)*

I'll tell you what reconciliation has meant. That killers walk free to breathe the same air as their victims. No more stories…you hear me? Your comic-book credo, your tiny travails *do…not…move me…*you understand?

JOSH rounds on PAPA.

You knew why you were there. What you were doing. You were a forty-five year old man. You knew. And if I didn't, *I should have.*

PAPA: *Nobody's interested in that kind of stuff any more! Nobody cares!* Don't you get it? Can't you see? Everyone's trying to survive. To eat. To move from one place to another. Your beloved blacks will be wiped out from AIDS within a decade, anyway! So much for the great liberation struggle. What a joke. You win your freedom then fuck yourself into extinction. You want justice? For who? You? Him? Me? It's too fucking late.

(Beat.)

JOSH: You were a superb soldier. But the thing that marks you out as unexceptional, as deluded, and identical to that long list of butchers who hide behind duty and dogma and state – is that every last one of you invested so much faith in your own fucking lie. Come now, Mr. Louw. See yourself with the cold eye you reserve for others: Why was George murdered? *In the name of what?* Can you answer me? Why?

PAPA: Because he was the enemy.

JOSH: *HE WASN'T THE ENEMY. YOU KNOW WHO THE ENEMY WAS. IT WAS ME!*

JOSH stuns PAPA's head on the desk.

PAPA: *(Groggily.)* You were a poes then. You still a poes. Now you've attacked me twice. If I shot you I'd have a case. So make it easy for me.

JOSH turns and moves away.

JOSH: You will answer for the death of George Jozana.

PAPA stands.

PAPA: He deserved what he got.

> *JOSH lunges at PAPA and grabs him in a headlock, forcing him down onto the table, then jams the pistol against his cheek.*

JOSH: I'm still fast. How does it feel. Captain? Your bowels nice and tight?

PAPA: Do it… *DO IT!*

> *JOSH steps back and aims the pistol – but cannot bring himself to shoot PAPA.*

Still fucking useless!

JOSH: *GIVE ME AN ANSWER!*

PAPA: To what? He used you! Did you ever think of that? Do you know what he was up to? *Did he ever tell you what he was really up to?*

JOSH: *I SHOT HIM LIKE AN ANIMAL IN THE BACK OF THE HEAD!*

PAPA: And now twenty years have gone. How will it serve this country if every sinner is punished in kind? I'll tell you: We'll be a nation of cripples! Look around you. Fuckall has changed. There's just a new bunch of cunts driving round in posh cars pocketing the bucks. Except now they're black. And good fucking luck to them. They're doing exactly what we did in forty-eight. I was born into a world that led me to do what I did. It was bad. But I did it. And now it's something I can't undo. I thought about that long before you crawled back to this country.

JOSH: What was it? What cancer was eating you? You never left me alone, did you?

> *JOSH bends down to PAPA's ear.*

Did you want to fuck me?

> *PAPA laughs.*

I carried him. Alone. Thirty kilometres he bled on my back. And you loved every little second, didn't you? Till you saw he'd beaten you at your own game.

PAPA: What is it with you? You like fantasy? You think you were innocent?

> *PAPA wrenches himself away from the table.*

What have you been doing since then? Huh? Tell me? What? Examining your bloody navel! So let me make it easy for you: when it came to the crunch the thing you cared about most was yourself. *He's dead, man. Dead. Understand?* His body was left to rot. With all the other corpses of war. Some of them your colour. That's the truth. You feel better? He was fighting for something. And so was I.

> *He flings the dossier up scattering its papers everywhere and rounds on JOSH.*

What have you ever fought for? I'll tell you: *a clear conscience.* No way, my boetie. Because whatever you do, you were there, and you were part of it. You will have to live with that for the rest of your life. *WE ARE LOCKED IN THAT PLACE! TOGETHER! FOREVER! FOR ETERNITY!* And when we face our maker, you'll get the same deal as me.

JOSH: I'm ready.

> *Someone BANGS LOUDLY on the shed and shouts:*

SIGNALMAN: *(Offstage.) Nantsi i yez!*

JOSH: In the end, Captain, it's simple.

> *(Beat.)*

I did a terrible thing for which I will suffer the rest of my life. But that was your plan. Your game. Your shabby project. Even if you didn't know it then, even if you haven't got the guts to admit it now. You saw something in me that got to you and when George made that baffling little link it fucked you up completely. In the end what drove you had nothing to do with fatherland, or valour, or duty. – It wasn't war. It was spite. –Whatever you feel you achieved in those thirty years of service for our country what you really are when all the guff is gone is a sad fucking monster who hauled me into his misery so he wouldn't be alone – the little Boere boy, crying for his mommy.

> *PAPA does not react. A TRAIN SHUNTS past, its light strobing the shed*

He had a daughter. She knows everything. She's in the country. And now so am I. It might have taken me twenty years to understand what happened in the bush, it might have taken the death of my father to claw me out of exile, but now I'm back I will pursue you if I have to, beyond the grave.

> *(Beat.)*

I've given the courts full disclosure. They may not be perfect, but for the moment, they're all I've got. And now I've found you, so can they. I'll leave *them* to decide if your motives were military or whether you were just driven by malice. If that fails there's still a civil suit. Or the press. Or the Hague. Or even a neat little posse of disaffected tsotsis who could do with a buck. And in the end… *I can always improvise.*

> *(Pause.)*

All those years ago as we rushed towards the rainbow, the gang of executioners tripped over themselves to proclaim their sins and snatch an easy absolution. But few soldiers came forward. At least now, whatever your fate – *and whatever mine* – the world will know what happened in Angola.

> *He approaches the desk, drops the pistol on the table. He does not take his eyes off PAPA.*

JOSH: 'A gift, from me to you.'

> *JOSH walks to the door.*

PAPA: Josh.

> *JOSH freezes.*

I confess.

> *JOSH turns to face PAPA.*

I envied you. More than any man I'd ever met. There was something in you that drove me senseless. Something about the way you did things...the way you spoke...your luck. It was all...effortless. You had everything I didn't.

(Beat.)

His death has nothing to do with that.

(Pause.)

JOSH: How do you sleep at night, Mr. Louw?

(Beat.)

PAPA: With a gun under my pillow.

(Pause.)

JOSH: May god show you mercy. Because I won't.

PAPA watches as JOSH exits and continues to stare at the spot. Finally, he reaches for his hipflask. There is a faint tinkle of MARIMBA. PAPA shivers. He turns to look at GEORGE... then turns away. There is the MAGNIFIED SOUND OF A STOPWATCH.

PAPA: In Africa, there is no god.

He jams the pistol in his mouth.

GUNSHOT / BLACKOUT.

SCENE THREE

Naulila, Angola. Scene of the execution. Two days later. The SOUND OF A WATERFALL. Hint of a hillock. LILY stands alone, searching the area. JOSH enters unseen. He watches LILY. She senses him and turns. She is surprised.

LILY: You came.

(Beat.)

JOSH: I kept my promise.

(Pause.)

He...gave me this...

JOSH takes a wad of wrapped cloth from his pocket.

90

…to give to you.

> *LILY takes it from him. Slowly, she unwraps the cloth. She takes the WOODEN FIGURINE from the cloth and stares at it, caresses it. She trembles.*

In the time I knew him he changed me. It was his parting shot. A last thumb in the eye for the enemy.

> *(Pause.)*

It's taken me twenty years. But I swore I would see you. That I would give you the token. Tell you how he went… and where it happened.

> *(Beat.)*

LILY: Who has this been for, Mr. Gilmore? You or me?

> *A TINKLE OF MARIMBA. Only JOSH seems to hear it. He indicates that she should follow him. They move to the spot where he executed George – the hillock. JOSH freezes, points down. There is A POWERFUL RUSH OF MARIMBA as GEORGE appears. He stares at LILY. As she speaks he moves to one side, watching her.*

You knew him. Not as well as you think. He was brave. A brilliant man. And he loved me. But he was never there.

GEORGE: Lily…

LILY: *(Not taking her eyes from figurine.)* When I was little, he came and went. He was very loving. But always fighting… fighting I think for control. Now I know why. The separations, they…must have hurt him badly. I spent my life waiting. And then one day he stopped coming.

> *GEORGE reaches out, strokes her briefly on the cheek, but she does not feel his touch.*

Many people loved him. But I didn't have a chance to do that, because he was married to the struggle. There were times I hated him for making that choice. For delivering himself into your hands. A killer bearing gifts.

> *She looks up at JOSH.*

Yet…he must have trusted you…to give you this.

(Beat.)

Now you know.

(Beat.)

The Truth Commission is long gone. But I never accepted its tenets of Christian forgiveness. Nor would my father. In this new democracy of ours people delight in renouncing the past. We no longer seem to cherish the things he died for. How those great men must be turning in their graves. What happened here has been forgotten, swallowed up by the world's need for a miracle.

(Beat.)

But one thing my father has taught me, is how to wait. In time, I'll decide how I'll honour his death. And maybe, one day, we'll find a way of preventing butchers like Papa Louw from hiding in their burrows.

(Beat.)

Butchers everywhere.

(Beat.)

As for you… We've met. That's happened. It's…*official.* You came. For that, I thank you. But what I sense you're really asking for I can never give you. Nor can any show of penance or commission of truth or court of law. In the end, we both know there is only one person you must talk to.

(Beat.)

LILY: My father.

(Beat.)

So stop running Mr. Gilmore. Pick up your burden, and carry it, like a man.

> *The light on LILY and JOSH fades down on them and up on GEORGE, who turns to the audience.*

GEORGE: I'm a child and I play a game with my mother:
'Mama, ukuba awuzange uhlangane nobaba, ngabe kwezekani?'
– 'What would have happened if you had not met my

daddy? Would I still be here?' Years pass and the questions change. 'What will happen here? Why are people dying?' But she always has the same answer, which never leaves me satisfied: *'Mtanami akekho umuntu ongavimba kwenzeke.'* Only once, does her answer satisfy me. It fills me with hope. My question comes on the last day I see her, the day I flee my country. I ask it in the way a grown man sometimes asks a parent when he needs to be a child again. *'Will there be justice?'* I ask her. *'Will there ever be justice for the dead, Mama?'* She holds my face in her hands and looks into my eyes, repeating the words: *'Mtanami akekho umuntu ongavimba kwenzeke'*:– 'No one can stop what must be.' Then…she does something she has not done for some time…

LILY appears beside him and kneels.

She talks… She talks to her ancestors. To the dead who are at peace… To her father…and his father…to our uncles… to the men of the Jozana family… And she asks…for intercession. She asks them to bring peace to the crumpled bodies in the earth.

MARIMBA build.

But then she asks for more. She asks them to leave a burden, a burden in the hearts of those who killed the innocent – a burden so heavy, that from its weight…there can be no escape…*but justice…* And she turns to me, her face wet with tears, her mouth in a broad smile, and we turn to our ancestors. And together…we talk…to the dead.

The MARIMBA SUDDENLY INTENSIFY as –

Nina! Bakomuhle Qosheme…

GEORGE and LILY, their voices swelling in power and purpose, praise their ancestors, by name:

LILY: Nina! Bakomuhle Qosheme…

GEORGE/LILY: Basiki Bekhwane Ebelebuthise Imanuba,
Kungabi Ndaba Zalutho…
Nina! Bolonze Lwenyosi Ezindala!

Ezingenisengothingo Lwe Nkosazana –
Nina! Bakosisila Sesakabula!
Esisavuze Emasimini Kwasfinhlava!
Nina! Bakomikilili Wakovilivili!
Ongximba Kamthwalo Usinda Amadoda!

GEORGE: *Jozana!*

LILY: *Jozana!*

GEORGE/LILY: *JOZANA!*

> *The light on LILY fades.*
>
> *GEORGE turns to JOSH, watching him. JOSH drops onto his knees. GEORGE walks slowly to JOSH, stopping behind him. For a moment the two men are still. Then JOSH raises a hand. GEORGE takes it.*
>
> *The MARIMBA REACH CRESCENDO.*
>
> *GEORGE climbs onto JOSH's back. As JOSH rises, the MARIMBA dissolve INTO KNOCKIN' ON HEAVEN'S DOOR...*
>
> *JOSH and GEORGE move slowly forward. They raise their eyes in unison, staring ahead. Then, slowly, they disappear into blackness.*

GLOSSARY OF ACRONYMS AND WORDS IN THE PLAY:

Abakhulu baka Jozana
I am coming, Jozanas

Amadlozi badimo
My ancestors

ANC
African National Congress

boetie
brother

brak
mongrel

onkundige esel
ignorant ass

ewe
yes

FAPLA
Angolan army

Goduka!
Get out of my sight!

isidenge
fool

Isitimela se ku gcina siyeza!
The last train is coming.

laaitie
child

Jusses
Jesus

bliksemse esel
Ignorant fool

mag die God van oorlog my krag gee.
May the God of war give me strength

Mtanami akekho umuntu ongavimba kwenzeke
No one can stop what must be

nantsi i yez!
Here it comes

isi khumbuso
a remembrance

marimba
African piano

meneer
mister

ovimbunyani
bloodsucker

Red Eye
Stalin organ rocket launcher

sithandwa sami, ngiya e-Angola
I am going to Angola.

South West Africa
Former Namibia

SWAPO
South West African People's Organisation
(Namibia's equivalent of the ANC)

Terr
terrorist

Xhosa
Language spoken by the Xhosas in east / west Cape.

Zulu
Language spoken by the Zulus whose major concentration is in Natal

The address to the ancestors by Lily and George was created by the author and the late Lindelaani Buthelezi who first played George, (some of the references very close to him), the loose translation of which is:

You – The people of Qosheme
Those who cut the fruit of the tree that heals.
Let this knowledge not be for nothing
You – guardians of the ancient bee
That brought us the sting of the queen.
You of Bakasisila – we who have struck with the axe
Who have bled into the fields of the Sfinhlava
You – who move with such power and speed
Those who can receive the burdens of men
Thank you
Thank you
THANK YOU.